# Mount Pleasant Cemetery

## An Illustrated Guide

# Mount Pleasant Cemetery

## An Illustrated Guide

### Mike Filey

A FIREFLY BOOK

First printing 1990

Copyright© 1990 by Mike Filey
Copyright© 1990 by Toronto Trust Cemeteries
Copyright© 1990 by Firefly Books Ltd.

All rights reserved.

The author and publisher are grateful for the
assistance given by Toronto Trust Cemeteries
towards the publication of this book.

Edited by Sarah Swartz, The Editorial Centre
Typesetting and mechanical art by On-line Graphics
Design by DUO Strategy and Design Inc.
Cover photograph by William Gee

**Canadian Cataloguing in Publication Data**

Filey, Mike, 1941–
  Mount Pleasant Cemetery

ISBN 0-920668-69-0

1. Mount Pleasant Cemetery (Toronto, Ont.) — History.
2. Mount Pleasant Cemetery (Toronto, Ont.) —
Guide-books. I. Title.

FC3097.61.F5 1990   917.13′541044   C90-095437-X
F1059.5.T6862M684 1990

A FIREFLY BOOK

Printed in Canada

# Table of Contents

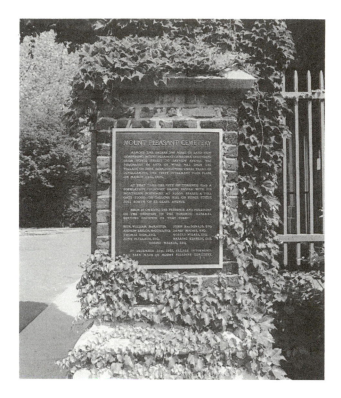

# Dedication

In memory of my father Jack Filey, and my grand-mother Martha Hatch (both in SECTION 51, LOT 89) and my aunt Peggy Gray (PLOT T, LOT 2439).

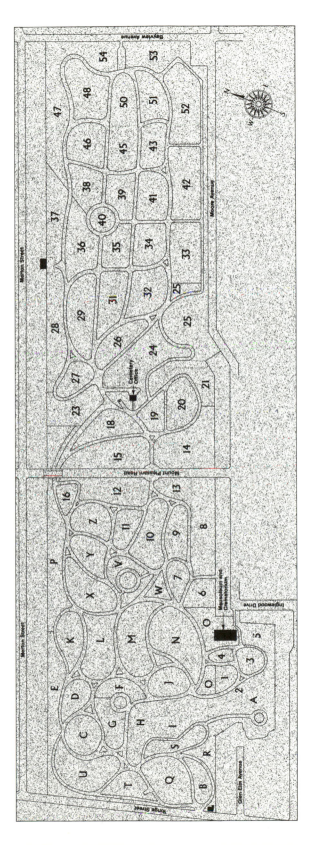

A Walking Tour of Mount Pleasant Cemetery

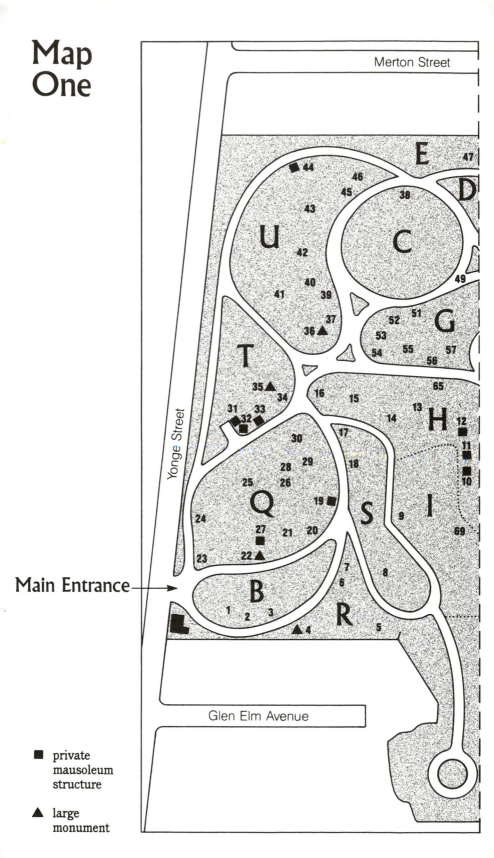

# Map
# One

Merton Street

E

47

U

44

46

45

43

38

D

C

42

40

41

39

49

37

36

52  51

G

53

55

57

54

56

T

65

35

34

16

15

13

31  33

32

14

H

12

30

17

11

28  29

18

10

25

26

Main Entrance →

24

Q

19

S

9

I

27

21  20

23

22

7

8

B

6

1

2  3

R

5

4

Yonge Street

Glen Elm Avenue

69

■  private
   mausoleum
   structure

▲  large
   monument

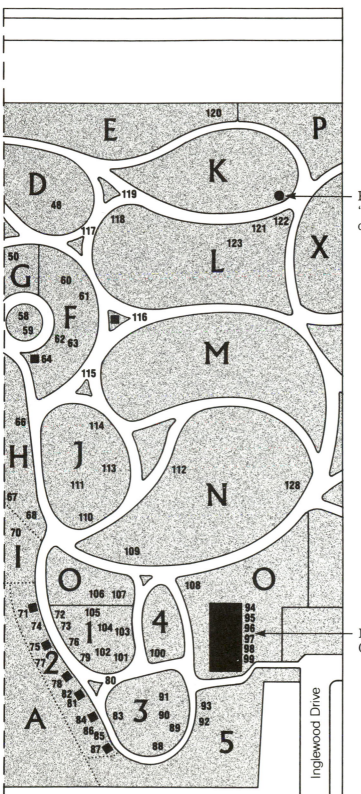

Plaque on boulder:
"Resting Place
of the Pioneers"

Mausoleum and
Crematorium Chapel

Inglewood Drive

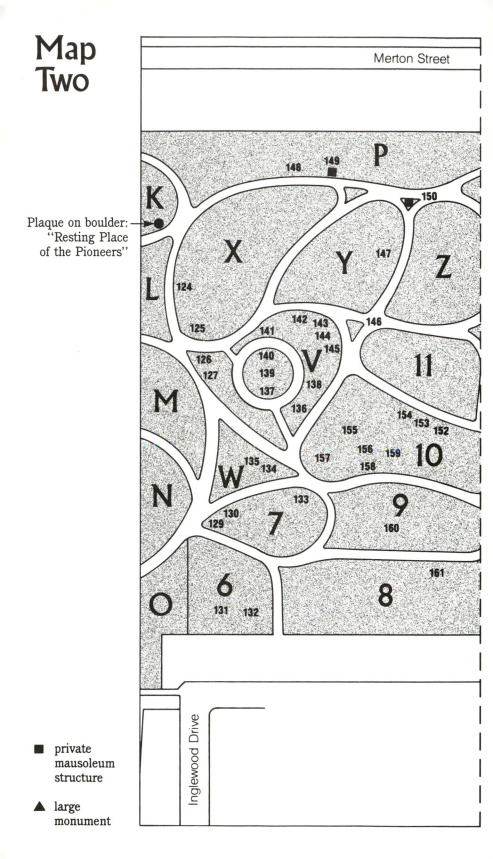

# Map Two

Merton Street

Plaque on boulder:
"Resting Place
of the Pioneers"

P

K

148  149

150

X  Y  147  Z

L  124

125  142 143
141  144
140  145  11
126  139  V
127  137  138

146

M  136

W  135  155  154 153 152
134  156 159  10
157  158

N  133
130  9
129  7  160

O  6  161
131  132  8

Inglewood Drive

■  private
mausoleum
structure

▲  large
monument

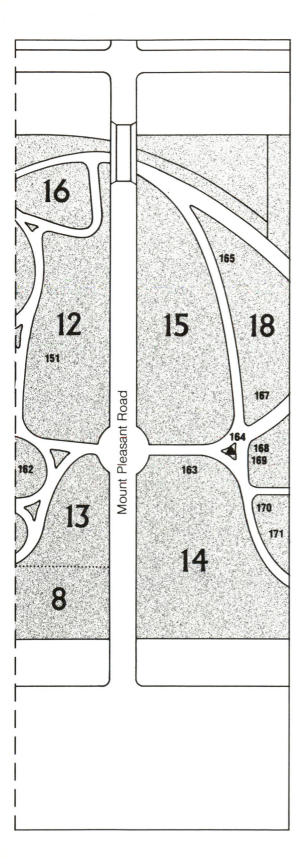

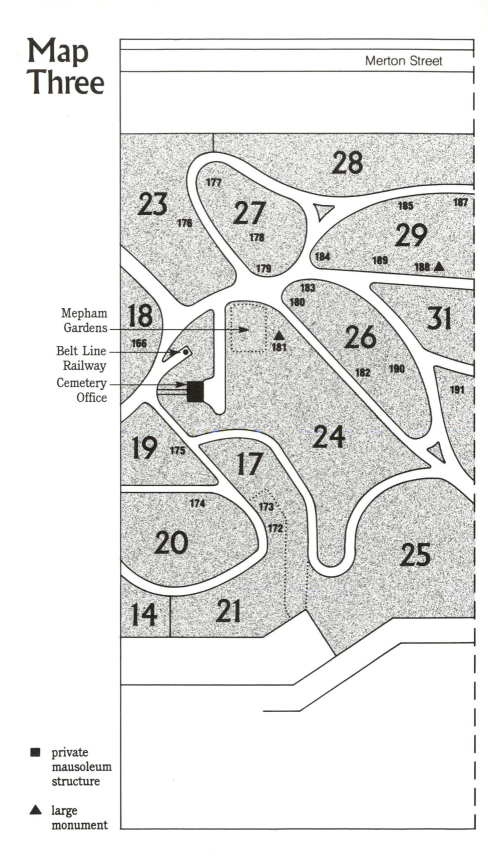

# Map Three

Merton Street

28

23
176

27
177
178
179

29
185    187
184    189    188 ▲

26
183
180

31

18
166

Mepham
Gardens

Belt Line
Railway

Cemetery
Office

181 ▲

182    190

191

24

19    175

17

173
172

20
174

25

14    21

■  private
   mausoleum
   structure

▲  large
   monument

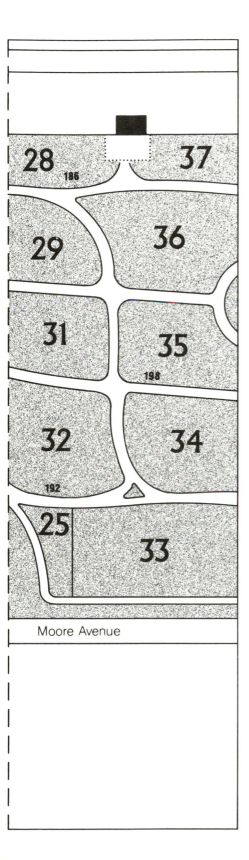

28   185

37

29

36

31

35   198

32   192

34

25

33

Moore Avenue

# Map
# Four

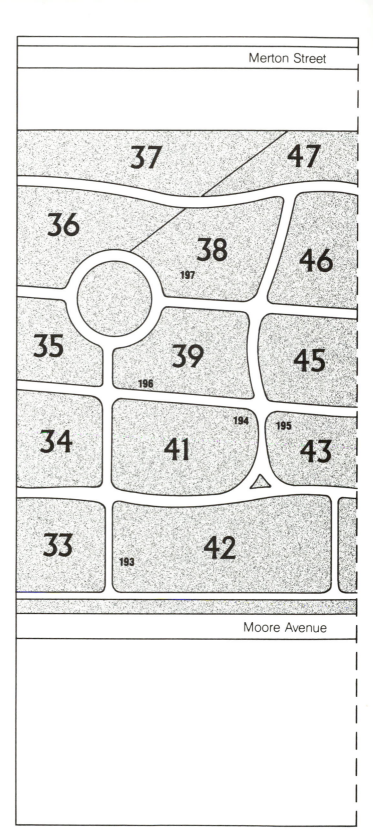

Merton Street

37

47

36

38

197

46

35

39

196

45

34

41

194

195

43

33

42

193

Moore Avenue

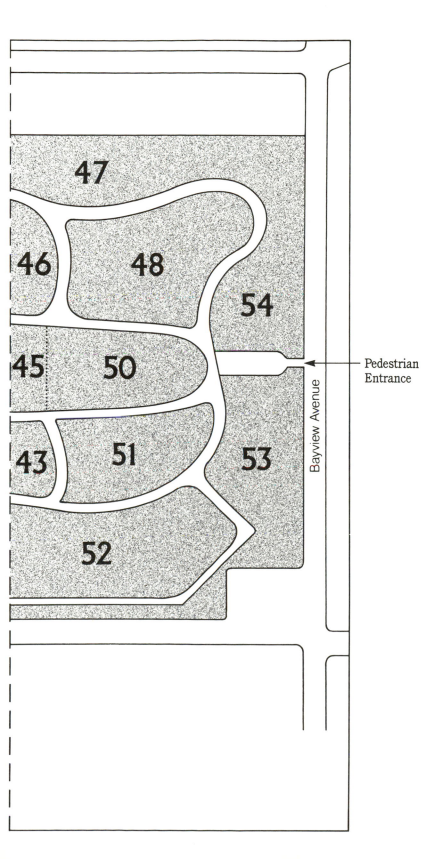

47

46

48

54

45

50

Pedestrian
Entrance

Bayview Avenue

43

51

53

52

# Preface

by R.D. Smith,
President and Chief Executive Officer
Toronto Trust Cemeteries

*I*n 1991, Mount Pleasant Cemetery will be 125 years old. This book is in part, a tribute to those years of history and all who played a part in that history.

All of us see the history of this city through different eyes, and our view of Mount Pleasant as a microcosm of Toronto's rich heritage is no different. In this book, Mike Filey colourfully describes the history of Mount Pleasant Cemetery through the stories of those interred there, Heinz Mueller through the changing faces of the monuments, Jack Radecki through the trees of Mount Pleasant Cemetery and Howard Clark through the eyes of someone who spent nearly half-a-century working within its grounds.

If you have ever visited Mount Pleasant or any of the other cemeteries operated by the Trust, you will know that they are amongst the finest in the world. Mount Pleasant Cemetery has many faces:

an extraordinary arboretum; floral and horticultural features rivaling the best public gardens on the continent; places of tranquility, reflection and remembrance; a place for passive recreation; architecture that is both pleasing and unique; a permanent record of our heritage to speak to future generations; a haven for wildlife; a resource centre for all levels of education; a commemorative facility where families and individuals can express the widest choice of ways to pay a tribute to a life lived. The tranquil beauty of the property is matched in excellence by the caring, compassionate service to families which all of us at Toronto Trust hold as our purpose.

Mount Pleasant Cemetery is the third cemetery established or operated by the Trustees and the second oldest that we currently administer. Our original cemetery, Potter's Field, was established by the Trustees in 1826 at what is now the northwest corner of Yonge and Bloor Streets. The remains of those buried were moved to the Necropolis and Mount Pleasant Cemetery and a plaque in each now commemorates the burial sites of those pioneers originally interred in that first non-profit, non-sectarian burying ground.

Toronto Trust Cemetery was created through a special act of the Legislative Assembly of Upper Canada in 1826. We are now in our 165th year of service to the citizens of Toronto and those communities nearby where we have facilities. We were created by public-spirited citizens, including Toronto's first Mayor, William Lyon Mackenzie, who identified and fulfilled a need for a burying ground for all,

17

irrespective of religion or race. Furthermore, they determined that no one should have proprietary interest in the organization. To achieve this, the initial funding was accomplished through public subscription with no individual or family permitted to contribute more than one dollar.

Today, the people of Toronto and surrounding communities are better served than in any large community anywhere in the world with respect to our facilities' role in the commemoration of life. This organization provides an extraordinary quality of service to the communities it serves, at no cost to the taxpayer.

We at Toronto trust are proud of our guardianship of the history and the beauty of Mount Pleasant Cemetery. We invite you to share in the wonder and enjoyment of the heritage it represents, as Mike Filey's insightful and colourful narrative guides you through the pages of Toronto history which have been carefully preserved in the commemoration of life at Mount Pleasant.

# Introduction

*I*knew I was in trouble when I was asked by the people at Toronto Trust Cemeteries to put together a book on the largest of the nine properties administered by this long established non-profit organization. Of course, this was not the kind of trouble that would sway me from doing the project, but rather the kind that was going to make it difficult for me to limit the work to anything under 168,000 entries.

That's the approximate number of interments there have been in Mount Pleasant Cemetery since Marion Martin's funeral cortege made its way northward up a narrow dirt trail called Yonge Street and through the small community of Deer Park to the newly laid out cemetery way back on March 13, 1876. And of the 168,000 whose final resting place is within the boundaries of the cemetery, it's a safe bet that there are almost as many stories that could be told.

However, in order to publish a book that could also be carried out of the store, what the reader will find in this particular volume is a collection of my own favourites and includes personalities who were well-known in their day as well as a selection of the "lesser lights". Collectively, they have made the story of our city and, yes one could also say the story of our province and country unique. Also included are several short stories that help the reader place this timeless place in some sort of time frame. And before I'm accused of being a male chauvinist, the fact there are relatively few females included in the guide simply emphasizes the way things used to be when women were subservient to men.

Be advised that the short (and in some cases not so short) vignettes that follow, rather than being a simple alphabetic register of personalities in Mount Pleasant Cemetery, have been assembled using a "tour" format with the main entrance gates off Yonge Street as the starting point of the tour.

Thanks to the work of landscape architect Engelhardt, who laid out the cemetery grounds more than a century ago, a leisurely ramble through Mount Pleasant will frequently result in covering the same ground twice. Never mind, it's a nice day for a stroll, so take your time. Another point: Because the cemetery developed from west to east, the vast majority of the "historic" personalities are found in the west part of the property.

By the way, time and acid rain have taken their toll and some of the headstones may be difficult to locate and decipher. The numbers on the map indicate approximately where the headstones are located and, while the stones may be difficult to find, rest assured, they are there. Again, be patient. And enjoy.

Mike Filey
June 14, 1990

*Yonge Street is still just a dirt road in this turn-of-the-century photo of Mount Pleasant Cemetery.*

*T*he origins of Toronto's Mount Pleasant Cemetery can be described as being older than the city itself.

In 1825, nine years before the Town of York became the City of Toronto, a small group of responsible community leaders - Thomas Carfrae, Jr., Peter Paterson, John Ewart, Thomas Morrison and Thomas Helliwell - convened a public meeting to discuss a problem that was beginning to create severe hardships for many of the town's citizens.

In those far-off days, the only authorized cemeteries in York, other than a few isolated family plots, were those that had been consecrated for adherents to either the Roman Catholic Church or Church of England.

Deceased citizens who were non-adherents to either of these religions, in addition to any indigents or visitors to the young community who had

*Early view of Mount Pleasant Cemetery*

the misfortune to die while in the town limits, were out of luck.

Thus it was that in 1826 a six-acre portion of the Elmsley farm, carefully selected because it was situated well north of the town limits at the northwest corner of Yonge Street and the Second Concession (a street better known today as Bloor Street), was purchased for the munificent sum of $300.

Burials in the new Potter's Field, as the cemetery was called, started almost immediately and by early 1855, more than 6,000 souls had been interred in the six-acre cemetery. However, coinciding with the expansion the community's suburban cemetery was the development of the adjacent Village of Yorkville. The cemetery was stifling Yorkville's growth, and before long the villagers were petitioning the provincial authorities to have Potter's Field closed and the remains removed to some other location.

The authorities acceded to the villagers' request, while at the same time enacting legislation which permitted the owners of Potter's Field to become a non-profit entity called the Toronto General Burial Ground Trust with the authority to acquire land for cemetery purposes. Members of the new Trust acted quickly to acquire a fifteen-acre cemetery on the west bank of the Don River at the end of Winchester Street that had been started a few years earlier by a private syndicate.

Unable to come up with the full $16,000 purchase price, three of the Trustees offered to lend the trust $15,000 while the trust itself contributed the remaining $1,000, all the non-profit organization had on hand.

The Necropolis, as the new cemetery was called, became part of the new Toronto General Burial Ground Trust on July 11, 1855. To comply with the Government's order that the old Potter's Field be closed and the remains therein reinterred elsewhere, the Trust offered the relatives of those buried in the old cemetery new plots in the Necropolis. Many families took advantage of the offer and soon most of the remains in Potter's Field were re-interred in the Trust's new cemetery on the banks of the Don.

As the population of the city continued to grow (42,000 inhabitants in 1855, 47,000 just a decade later), so too did the number of "dear departed". As a result, it wasn't long before the capacity of the Necropolis too was being taxed. Anticipating future needs, the Trust began actively seeking out additional land on which to develop a new cemetery in 1872.

One year later, a 200- acre farm on the east side of Yonge Street, in the Third Concession from the Bay, Township of York was purchased for $20,000. At a meeting of the Trustees called to confirm the acquisition of this new property, described at the meeting in more familiar terms as being several hundred yards north of the little community of Deer Park, it was agreed that the

**MOUNT PLEASANT**
**CEMETERY**

third of the Trust's non-sectarian cemeteries would be called Mount Pleasant.

The responsibility for laying out the new cemetery was assigned to Henry Engelhardt, a German-born landscape designer whom the Trustees hired, based his successful experiences developing public grounds, gardens and cemeteries in various American and Canadian cities.

Engelhardt's concept for the Trust's new cemetery would follow the newly emerging "landscape style" that was gaining prominence south of the border. He drew on Boston's innovative Mt. Auburn Cemetery for many of his ideas.

Work started at the Yonge Street end of the property. Over the next few months, Engelhardt supervised the transformation of ordinary farm fields into a park-like setting complete with trees, shrubs, pathways and even a small lake. The first interments in the new cemetery were the few unclaimed remains from the old Potter's Field that had not been removed to the Necropolis.

As Engelhardt's work progressed, the emerging Mount Pleasant Cemetery became such a departure from the ordinary type of burial ground that it soon became a featured item in the city's daily newspapers. The cemetery was perceived to be an attraction of such uniqueness that city souvenir guide books made a point of recommending a visit into the countryside north of the city to witness its wonders: "No visit to Toronto will be complete without a visit to Mount Pleasant Cemetery. The cars of the Metropolitan Street Railway run right to the main entrance".

On the afternoon of November 4, 1876, a little more than two years after the trustees purchased the 200-acre Yonge Street farm, the public was invited to attend the official opening of Toronto's new Mount Pleasant Cemetery.

# Recollections of
# Mount Pleasant Cemetery

by Howard Clark, former General Manager,
Toronto General Burying Grounds, from 1965 to 1977

*A*lthough I had previously worked while a student at Prospect and Pine Hills Cemeteries, my first memories of Mount Pleasant date back to the early 1930s. At that time, working hours for the men on the grounds were from seven in the morning until five, six days a week. The only non-working days were Good Friday and Christmas Day. Every Sunday, two members of the office staff were on duty from 9:00 a.m. until 10:00 a.m. Coffee breaks were still unknown for the outside workers and anyone taking time off for one in the 1930s would probably have been fired on the spot.

Men doing the heaviest type of work were paid at the rate of fifty cents per hour while others, such as grass cutters, were paid forty cents per hour. No deductions were made for unemployment insurance, health insurance premiums, O.H.I.P., union dues, etc. There were no "fringe" benefits whatsoever and the men were paid in cash every second Friday. A few would not show up for work again until the following Tuesday morning, broke and unrepentant. Although there was no formal pension plan as such, it was the custom of management and the Trustees to provide light work for employees no longer capable of performing their normal jobs. Depending on the circumstances, some employees were granted pensions.

All graves were dug with picks and shovels and most grass cutting was done with hand mowers. I can still visualize as many as twenty men on their hands and knees all day long, trimming around monuments with sheep shears. Many

**MOUNT PLEASANT
CEMETERY**

*View of Mount Pleasant Cemetery c.1900*

of the men working on the grounds in those days were really unforgettable characters.

Until the early 1950s, the Mount Pleasant Cemetery office occupied part of the building at 1643 Yonge Street with the remainder of the building being used as the head office of the Trustees. Outside the building was a bell tower. Until the late 1930s a rope connected this to the office. It was someone's duty in the office to toll the bell as each funeral procession entered the gates, one ring for every car in the procession.

During the Second World War, labour was very scarce. We hired policemen, firemen, school teachers, soldiers, sailors, airmen, women and almost anyone capable of walking, on a part time basis to work until darkness set in. I think it was in 1943 that the grass throughout most of the cemetery grew to a height of two to three feet and was eventually cut with scythes, sickles and horse drawn mowers where possible.

26

Until about 1935, quite a large pond existed in what is now the west glen into which the storm water from the area of Eglinton and Bathurst drained. A six foot concrete storm sewer was built through this area. Clean earth fill was brought in from neighbouring excavations for which twenty-five cents per cubic yard was paid to the excavating contractors. Later, the stream in the east glen was picked up by the same storm sewer and filled in to a depth of fifteen to twenty feet.

The men who did the actual digging of the graves were Irish for the most part and called themselves "slay carpenters". Two grave lots were available for $48 and the standard interment fee was $12.

A Trustee visited and inspected each cemetery once a month. Trustees met each week. Three Trustees constituted a quorum, and I do not recall a meeting being cancelled due to lack of a quorum. All cheques for goods and services had to have a Trustee's signature until the early 1960s.

*The Pond c.1900*

All entombment rights in the mausoleum had been sold by 1930. It was much later when niches, additional crypts and the crematorium were installed.

A private telephone line had been installed in the 1920s to enable the office to contact a foreman or the superintendent on the grounds between Yonge Street and Mount Pleasant Road. The wires and call boxes were placed on trees. However by 1930, this system had been done away with and only a few call boxes remained on the trees.

Prior to 1935, the only trees standing east of the Belt Line right-of-way was the large grove of red oak close to the northern boundary, most of which are still there.

During the Second World War, many residents of Leaside had vegetable gardens - kind of a "Victory" garden - on the land adjacent to Bayview Avenue. The Trustees had the land prepared and a water system installed. Thousands of cubic yards of clean earth fill were hauled and graded by the contractor, free of charge, from the Yonge Street subway on to the sections east of the Belt Line right-of-way.

The bridge built in 1930 over the old Belt Line needed a great deal of repair work and, consequently, was demolished when the Trustees acquired the right-of-way from the city in the 1950s.

From the opening of Mount Pleasant Cemetery in 1876, successive management had a policy of acquiring and planting as many trees and shrubs as possible that were hardy in this climate. The result has been that Mount Pleasant Cemetery is the closest thing to a tree arboretum in Ontario.

# The Monuments of Mount Pleasant Cemetery

by Heinz Mueller, Stone Mason and Stone Carver,
President, Wholesale Lettering and Carving Limited, Toronto.
Assisted by Benita DesRoches.

"*S*how me your cemetery, and I shall tell you what society you live in."

This is certainly true of Mount Pleasant Cemetery in Toronto. If one is an historian, Mount Pleasant is indeed a treasure house to explore. A picture of societal changes in Toronto over the past 150 years is truly written in stone within these gates. The gentle hilly terrain, the majestic old trees and the historic expertly crafted family monuments all contribute to the peaceful atmosphere which makes Mount Pleasant one of the most beautiful cemeteries in North America. The memories of those who have gone before us seem to live on in this sanctuary of remembrance. Let us embark on a journey into the living cemetery.

Our exploration must begin within the oldest section of Mount Pleasant Cemetery which is found closest to Yonge Street. Touring these sections, one can see that Toronto had a well established society in place before the turn of the century. Note that the graves were located in sizable family lots, adorned by generally large impressive monuments. These monuments served complete family units - sometimes up to twenty different family members. These stones generate an imposing image of solidity and permanence, much as an old country estate does. When exploring these old sections, one must remember that the granite industry in Canada was in its infant stage. Although stone quarries were operating, they mainly produced paving blocks. Very few stone saws existed and polishing was extremely

**MOUNT PLEASANT CEMETERY**

difficult. The production in Canada of round polished columns common to this section was impossible. Indeed most of these large polished granite monuments boasting beautiful spires or columns adorned with urns, were imported from Scotland and Northern Ireland. They were delivered from the boat to the cemetery by hand and erected using block and tackle, since cranes were as yet non-existent. Even most of the granite for the impressive Eaton mausoleum (particularly the columns and expertly carved Corinthian capitals) was imported from Scotland. In general, monument bases were constructed of limestone quarried in Kingston or the Niagara Peninsula. Marble used in this section originated in New England, especially from New Hampshire. Of interest is the fact that a number of zinc monuments were produced locally and can be discovered in Mount Pleasant Cemetery.

The marble, limestone and unpolished granite monuments of the time were shaped and carved completely by hand in Toronto and they are a

*Monument setting by block and tackle.*

*A view of the beautiful columns and Corinthian capitals found on the EATON mausoleum. (see #87)*

credit to the craftsmen of the British Isles. It was at this time that highly skilled stone masons arrived in Toronto, and opened up granite sheds bearing Scottish names such as McIntosh, Creber and McIntyre. The fine work which these craftsmen produced leaves the impression that people of this period were individuals; very seldom are any two monuments the same. The memorial style was mainly Victorian with heavy solid bases, but there were also some Renaissance and Gothic styles. With the exclusion of a few sculpted angels, there are no sculptures of saints, as in the Catholic cemeteries. Not to be missed are a number of Renaissance styled ladies of sorrow carved in marble imported from Italy. These sculptures can be found encased in beautiful gazebo style monuments constructed of imported granite columns, and their effect is quite beautiful.

Unquestionably, monuments were designed with much individuality but the consistent use of symbolism as ornamentation was also prevalent.

**MOUNT PLEASANT
CEMETERY**

The following list of some symbolic interpretations is helpful when viewing these older memorials.

**Columns:** Broken - a person has passed away in the prime of his life
Complete - signifies that life has been completed
Urn on top - a symbol of death
Shroud on urn - a funerary sign meaning burial
**Acanthus leaf:** very common in the cemetery especially on corners of capitals, holding up globes, etc.,
- symbol of peace in the Garden of Eden
**Palm:** symbol of peace, also of resurrection, forever lasting life
**Ivy:** symbol of immortality because it stays green forever
**Anchor:** used in the catacombs, anchored in the Christian belief which even death cannot change, symbol of hope
**Clover:** the trinity, symbol of the Irish
**Hands:** One hand - the hand of God
Two hands - holy matrimony
**Laurel:** symbol of victory
**Celtic cross:** Irish (dear to the Church of Scotland)
**Grapes:** God's care, blood of Christ, last supper
**Eye in triangle:** eye of God in the Trinity, all seeing, all knowing
**Alpha omega:** very old sign used in second century, first and last letter of alphabet (Greek), beginning and end of life
**R.I.P.:** short form for Requiescat in pace (Rest in Peace)
**Star with 5 corners:** the Pentagram, old Greek sign for magician, symbol of the golden rule, the deceased is under protection of Christ
**Olive branch** (with dove): peace, symbol of safety which the dove brought to Noah after the flood
**Cross and crown:** victory with Christ over death
**Lily:** purity
**Ladder:** scale of Perfection

Also recognizable in the older section are the monuments of many successful merchants such as Messrs. Michie and Fulton.

We also observe many military memorials. This profession was very respected at the time and therefore high social status was designated. One particularly stunning monument honours officers killed in the Northwest Rebellion at Batôche, Saskatchewan in the late 1800s. The carving on this monument is exquisite. As you leave this oldest section of Mount Pleasant, bear in mind the consistency of Anglo Saxon surnames, with only a smattering of North European and French surnames to be found. Such was society at the time.

*Expert carving is found on this memorial honouring two officers killed in the North-West Rebellion of 1885. (see #66)*

**MOUNT PLEASANT CEMETERY**

*A beautiful memorial from the 1930's exhibiting the continental European influence. (see #108)*

In the central sections between Yonge Street and Mount Pleasant Road, the time period leading up to the First World War is largely represented. Imports are still widespread, but much more rough granite is now imported from Barre, Vermont. Unpolished monuments cut by the local craftsmen are common. Because of this, much lead lettering is utilized to create a contrast between inscription and the unpolished stone. The memorial styles are still predominantly Victorian with a slightly higher ratio of Gothic styles appearing. Section N is notable for its abundance of two grave lots (much smaller than in previous years), characterized by scroll type marble monuments.

However in the section west of Mount Pleasant Road you will discover a big change, because in the late 1920s and early 1930s the monument imports from Scotland came to an end. The quarries in Scotland were becoming exhausted just as the granite industry in Canada (particularly in the granite centre of Quebec) was becoming more mechanized. It became uneconomical to shape monuments by hand and consequently many of the large granite sheds in Toronto closed and retained smaller operations for lettering, carving and sculpture work. Note the more standardized look of these monuments -

eight or ten inches in thicknesses and horizontal, rather than vertical, dimensions. During this period, Italian craftsmen such as Marini, Ranzetti and Temporale began arriving in Toronto to pursue their craft. Likewise, German sculptors like Schnoen and Hahn also began making their presence felt. A good example of the German sculptor Hahn's work is found in the Cutten monument (PLOT O, LOT 18), evidenced by the two female nudes seated on a bench in classical style. At this point, the Victorian norm is declining as more Renaissance and Gothic styles emerged. The painful effects of the 1930s upon Toronto society are also recognizable in the small inexpensive monuments with rock sides made out of soft Georgia granite. Ornamentation and inscription is simple and to a minimum. Family lots in these sections are clearly smaller indicating that society was becoming more mobile. Although Anglo Saxon surnames still prevail, the recent immigration of the time is documented by more Dutch, German and Scandinavian surnames.

*Large family monument constructed of granite from Barre, Vermont.*

**MOUNT PLEASANT
CEMETERY**

*Excellent example of the Celtic Cross displaying both Irish and Welsh influences.*

Let us cross over Mount Pleasant Road into yet newer sections of the cemetery. In the area between Mount Pleasant Road and the cemetery office you can see the popular steeled monuments in the majority interspersed with more polished monuments, as this option had now become less expensive. Columns, spirals and other facets of Victorian style have been completely replaced by some Renaissance but mainly Gothic design styles. Emblematic ornamentation (service badges, Masonic symbols, crests, etc.) is common here and floral ornamentation has increased. Mount Pleasant's first appearances of religious ornamentation (Christ, Mary, praying hands) can be found. Generally, monuments are quite plain featuring rock sides. Examples of early serpentine top monuments can also be found in this section. A large family monument's significance as a status symbol in Anglo Saxon society has been replaced by alternative methods of remembrance, such as the practice of donating to charity in memoriam. Consequently, the lot sizes are now smaller. In the older parts of plots A, I and S and east of the cemetery office, we enter a truly multicultural society. Here we find Ukrainians, Poles, Russians, Estonians, Japanese, Vietnamese, Greeks, Italians, Chinese and many others. The impact of immigration into the Toronto area has made its presence known in Mount Pleasant Cemetery. These ethnic groups have all brought their own unique rich cultural backgrounds with them. This can be witnessed by the different memorial traditions alive in these newer sections.

*This Estonian community feature is located in the centre of the Estonian section.*

Before some of these traditions are discussed, however, one should be aware of several fundamental changes which have recently shaped and are still shaping Mount Pleasant Cemetery. Regulations stipulated that soft stones (such as marble and limestone) were no longer permitted. This is a practical consideration, as softer stones are not suited to our northern climate conditions. In an effort to improve the quality of memorials, rock side monuments are not allowed. All sides on monuments have to be finished. In order to offer alternatives to the higher costs of monuments, shared monuments have been introduced in which different families own and use each side of the monument. For this same reason, you can see more flat markers in the ground or mounted on fieldstone walls. As cremation increased, the cemetery responded to this need by creating special features - sundials, flower beds, etc. In Section 40 can be found the Scattering Garden - cremated remains are interred in a wooded area and the names of those persons buried here are commemorated on bronze plaques on a memorial feature. The effect achieved here is one of a peaceful return to nature. Once again, it should be mentioned that because of our mobile society and smaller family unit, the need for large family lots has diminished.

*The memorial feat found in the Scatt Garden.*

As of the 1960s a collage of nationalities has emerged in Mount Pleasant Cemetery. The preponderance of Anglo-Saxon surnames is no longer a given. Some of the first ethnic groups represented here are Ukrainians, Polish, Greeks and the Estonians. Symbolic ornamentation is important among these groups, but the symbols seen in these newer sections differ greatly from the list of symbols outlined previously. For instance, many Ukrainian memorials feature the Orthodox cross or the common use of wheat as ornamentation. Wheat means life and broken wheat means life is discontinued (cut down in the prime of life). The use of Mary as a religious feature is also common, for there have been many visions of Mary reported in the Ukraine. The trident is the national emblem of the Ukraine and the Kalyna is recognized to be the official flower of the military. Many designs taken from the beautiful garments of the Ukraine are adapted to memorial design, and since designs vary from region to region in the Ukraine much personal meaning can be attached to the use of such ornamentation.

The Polish people have two strong cultural symbols which are commonly used. The Black Madonna from Czestochowa and the Polish eagle and are in evidence throughout the cemetery.

The Greeks favour many symbols from antiquity: the laurel wreath, the Greek key, many carvings of ancient columns and the popular acanthus leaf. The Estonians are well represented in Section 46. Actually many of these interments were transferred from Westminster Cemetery after Westminster was forced to undertake flood control measures because of Hurricane Hazel. This Estonian section is impressive and shows great individuality. The depiction of the sun as giver of life is common here. As with the Ukrainians, much of the ornamentation on these monuments is adapted from weaving patterns and designs specific to Estonian culture.

*Above and opposite: These impressive Chinese memorials feature pagoda rooftops and Fu Chu Dogs.*

Some of the very newest sections of Mount Pleasant Cemetery are characterized by the preponderance of immigration from the Pacific - Japanese, Vietnamese, Chinese and especially those from Taiwan and Hong Kong. With their ancient rich cultures, they present to us entirely different symbols and ornamentation once again. The distinctive fu-chu dogs (lions) protected the castle of the emperor in ancient times and are today used as protection for the grave. Many of these beautiful free-standing fu-chu dogs were carved by sculptor, Siggy Puchta. The pagoda roof is a familiar feature seen in this section. Originally pagoda roofs were constructed in Asia to be earthquake-resistant and this architectural style has been carried into burial customs.

Chinese culture is rich with symbolic ornamentation. A few examples are the dragon sign of the king and used to signify the male, and the phoenix sign for happiness, used to signify the female. The water lily (lotus) represents purity, the bamboo means integrity and gentility and the pine tree symbolizes sincerity, honesty and generosity. Often noticeable on Chinese monuments is the distinctive Chinese key of which Mount Pleasant Cemetery bears many good examples. As one views the Oriental monuments, you notice that certain monuments have their inscriptions actually painted in. These are in fact Vietnamese memorials. Vietnamese culture uses these colours to denote either life or death: red paint indicates that the person is still living and green paint reveals that the person has passed away.

There are numerous other traditional symbols to be found on modern memorials and there most likely will continue to be as our multicultural base broadens. It is interesting to observe that even the colour of granite selected is often culturally based. For example, the Chinese prefer red granites from India, while the Ukrainians prefer black granite from Africa. This is, of course, not the rule, but is often noticeable as you stroll through Mount Pleasant Cemetery.

The relatives of those resting in Mount Pleasant are always observable, and it is fitting that a few words be dedicated to some of the varied customary

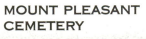

practices and traditions that take place in the cemetery. For example, in Vietnamese culture selecting the date to erect the stone must be done according to the ancient horoscope. It must incorporate the day of birth or of death. The Chinese celebrate the ancient custom of placing money (facsimiles) on top of their memorials so that the deceased may have a better time in the afterworld.

Many cultures have rites in which the grave is visited on special days and certain traditions are observed. Two days are very special for the Chinese community: Ching Ming Day (Spring) and Chung Ying Day (Fall). These days are celebrated with a family meal consisting of special foods (including barbecued pork and fruit) at the grave site. The Greek/Macedonian culture also has a traditional family meal at the grave site in which candles are lit and the soul of the deceased is prayed for. This takes place one year after the death. The Ukrainian community has traditions which date back to pagan times. Historically, the Ukrainians would have a

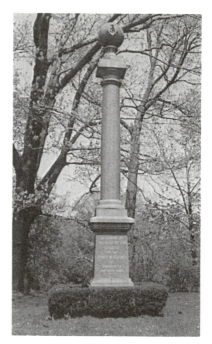

*FREEMASONS OF TORONTO*
*memorial, erected at the turn of*
*the century. (see #22)*

traditional meal at the gravesite followed by celebration in the form of music and dance. This tradition over time has refined itself to a more simple family meal in which a traditional embroidered tablecloth is laid upon the grave and traditional foods, including superbly painted eggs, are enjoyed by the family while the name of the deceased is called out intermittently. This meal takes place one week after Easter.

Anglo-Saxon remembrance services take place regularly throughout the year also and as most of these are group celebrations, they are quite impressive. Decoration Day is observed regularly in June and of course Remembrance Day in November is an important event for the entire community. Many veterans' services occur throughout the year. For instance the 48th Highlanders hold their special remembrance the Saturday before November 11th at the site of their War Memorial. Service clubs such as the Salvation Army, Masons, Elks Society, Trinity Estonian Society, St. Andrew's Society and many more honour their deceased on special dates. Celebrated holidays such as Easter, Christmas, Mother's Day and Father's Day, are always special also and many relatives like to have the unveilings of their monuments occur for these events.

Today's Mount Pleasant Cemetery is a peaceful oasis for those who have lived before us, but also a welcoming respite from our fast paced world where one can take a few moments for quiet reflection or simply enjoy the park-like atmosphere of the beautiful grounds. Mount Pleasant Cemetery is host to a wide variety of different activities. At any given time, you may spot a school group intently discussing the trees and botanical life of the property, cyclists or joggers enjoying a refreshing tranquil escape from urban life or someone just relaxing beside the beautiful waterfall and pond.

Mount Pleasant Cemetery is an active part of our community today and a noble tribute to our community of yesterday.

**MOUNT PLEASANT
CEMETERY**

# The Trees and Shrubs of Mount Pleasant Cemetery

*Japanese Katsura Tree*

by Jack Radecki, Arborist, Toronto Trust Cemeteries

*O*ne of the finest tree collections in North America is to be found in Mount Pleasant Cemetery.

The landscaping at Mount Pleasant Cemetery follows the basic plan first developed for the property in the late nineteenth century: to provide an arboretum for the enjoyment of the public. Practically every tree that will grow in this climate is found here. To make identification easier, many trees bear small signs with both their botanical and common names.

The hundred of varieties of trees in Mount Pleasant Cemetery form two groups: pioneer or native and introduced trees. These two groups range from the rare Oriental smooth leaf elm (in

Plots G, J, L and Section 28) and Babylonian willow from the Middle East (along Yonge Street) to oak trees that were mature when Mount Pleasant Cemetery was founded in 1873 (Plots H, I, Q and Section 2). As trees are removed due to old age, disease or safety, an effort is made to replant with a species that will complement the arboretum. Rare trees are obtained from many sources, and come from as far as England. For those who are interested, an arboretum guide is available at the cemetery office. The guide includes an alphabetical index and map showing tree locations, making it easy to find all specimens.

The first thing you will notice about the trees here is their shape: pyramidal (conical), cylindrical (columnar), spindle shaped, ovoid, ellipsoid or blobose. They may also be described as umbrella shaped (white elm), weeping (weeping willow), flag form (white pine, the shape is caused by prevailing winds), layered (not typical of cemetery trees) or irregular (old oaks). Less apparent is their rate of growth. Some, such as the Carolina poplar (Plots

*Camperdown Elm*

M, N and Z), can reach a height of sixty feet in twenty years. Others, such as the white oak (Plots I, Q and Y), will take a century to achieve the same stature. The average age of the pioneer trees in Mount Pleasant Cemetery is 130 years and of the introduced trees sixty-five years. Many specimens have been named Heritage Trees, indicating both their condition and venerable age.

Foliage characteristics vary from the purple Schwedler maples (Plots H, R and Z) of the Norway maple family to the puffy seed clouded Japanese Katsura tree (Plot I, L, O and Sections 20 and 52) that look as though they belong in an Oriental print.

The Ginkgo biloba, a member of the most primitive living tree family (it is thought to be the

*Copper Beech*

46

*Weeping Mulberry*

oldest "living fossil" having survived unchanged for some 200 million years), is unusual in having separate male and female trees. Both genders may be found in Mount Pleasant Cemetery (Plot U).

Some trees, like the prized sweetgum (Plot V) from the southern U.S.A. are difficult to grow in this climate. Because of the maturity of Mount Pleasant's tree collection, there are several sheltered locations for such sensitive plants.

Over the years, a wide variety of fruit and nut trees has been introduced, attracting birds and small animals. The oak, chestnut, hickory, walnut, pear, plum, apple and crabapple trees nourish chipmunks, squirrels, cardinals, tanagers, orioles, blue jays, warblers, robins, finches, juncos and many others.

**MOUNT PLEASANT
CEMETERY**

*Smoke Bush*

Complementing its treasure trove of trees, Mount Pleasant Cemetery has a vast range of flowering and coloured foliage shrubs as well as herbaceous perennials.

Some of the trees in Mount Pleasant Cemetery are famous simply through association. Two such trees are the maples (one red, one sugar) (Plot X, Lot 12) where Alexander Muir, who wrote the patriotic song "The Maple Leaf Forever", is buried. These trees were already there when, two weeks after Muir's death on June 26, 1906, our city fathers were debating whether or not to pay the $185 price tag on the lot - which they considered nothing short of highway robbery!

In Mount Pleasant Cemetery you will find a number of tulip trees, a 200-year-old pioneer red oak, a pendant silver linden from England, a Swiss stone pine and what is believed to be the largest Asian elm in Canada. There is also a cucumber tree (Plot V), whose cup shaped flowers produce cucumber shaped fruits.

The variety of flowers produced by Mount Pleasant's trees and shrubs is vast, ranging from minute and inconspicuous to some of the most beautiful flowers produced by any plant. Flowering generally begins in late March (red and silver maples, Cornelian cherry) and runs right through until November, when the witch hazel is still in bloom. In the intervening months one can see such exquisite blossoms as the magnolia in late April, the rhododendron in mid May, the peonies in early June, and the Pee Gee Hydrangea in August.

One way of exploring the arboretum is by walking through the property along the paved roadways and wood chip covered path that links the Vale of Avoca in the south western part of Mount Pleasant Cemetery with Moore Park Ravine in the south eastern section. Blue walkway signs make it easy to follow.

Trees are invaluable to any city, not only for their beauty and shade but also for the life-supporting oxygen they produce. They protect the soil from erosion. They provide food and shelter for wildlife. They are a cheaper source of air conditioning. Just three trees planted around a house can lower its temperature by as much as ten to fifteen degrees. A tree population heavily influences what will grow on a property. The protection of a mature arboretum enables the cultivation of plants which otherwise would not survive our climate. The trees and shrubs of Mount Pleasant Cemetery require constant care, but the return on all that goes into maintaining this bounty is incalculable.

**MOUNT PLEASANT
CEMETERY**

# A Walking Tour of Mount Pleasant Cemetery

*P*lease note that the order of this section corresponds to the maps on pages 8-15. It begins at the Yonge Street entrance. An alphabetical listing of the notable people and sites in the cemetery, along with corresponding page numbers, follows:

**MOUNT PLEASANT
CEMETERY**

# David See

# #1, plot B, sec 7, lot 7

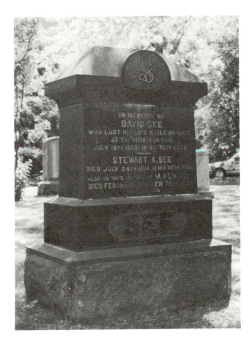

*E*arly in the morning of July 10, 1902, members of the Toronto Fire Department turned out to fight a fire that had erupted in an old storage building on George Street just south of Front Street owned by the P. McIntosh Feed Company. The three-storey structure, packed full of straw and hay, had been used for a time as a stable for the horses used by the Toronto Street Railway Company. By the time the first few firemen arrived on the scene, it was obvious that the blaze was going to be a bad one. Without warning, the east wall collapsed onto George Street burying three firemen beneath the tons of brick and mortar. By the time their colleagues were able to dislodge the trio of bodies,

David See, Harry Clarke and Adam Kerr were dead. Less than five minutes later there was another muffled explosion, and this time the south wall collapsed into a small laneway where two more firefighters, Walter Collard and Fred Russell, were last seen. Again there was frantic digging. This time, the firemen uncovered two more mangled bodies. In total, five firemen had been killed fighting the stubborn McIntosh fire.

On Sunday, July 13, following a moving service in St. James Cathedral, the longest funeral procession in the city's history moved west along King Street and north on Yonge to Mount Pleasant Cemetery where the remains of the five young men were interred. While two of the young men were originally buried in other areas of the cemetery, by September of 1903 all five were resting as they worked - together. Firemen See is in PLOT B, SEC 7, LOT 7, Clarke in PLOT B, SEC 8, LOT 7, Collard in PLOT B, SEC 8, LOT 6, Russell, PLOT B, SEC 6, LOT 7 and Kerr in PLOT B, SEC 16, LOT 6. The McIntosh tragedy remains the worst loss of firefighters' lives in the long and gallant history of the Toronto Fire Department.

 # William Brookman
## #2, plot B, sec 12, lot 3

*T*his unique memorial with its anchor motif marks the final resting place of the Rev. William Brookman who was born in England. In the late 1840s, he arrived in Toronto after a number of years in the East Indies. He became an ordained Church of

England Minister, but left the Church of England to set up his own Church of the Baptized Believers. On his request, his Church was dissolved upon his death which occurred at 43 Charles Street East on April 2, 1907. The anchor carved on the headstone symbolizes Brookman's long tenure as Chaplain to the Navy Veterans.

 # Wilfrid Burton Tait

## # 3, plot B, sec 16, lot 1

*B*orn in Blyth, Ontario, Tait had joined the Royal Flying Corps after completing his schooling at the University of Toronto Schools. The young man, who lived in the family home at 620 Spadina Avenue, had enlisted in October of 1917 and taken his flight training with the corps in Texas. He had recently been assigned as a flying instructor at the R.A.F.'s Leaside Camp and Airdrome, located on the east side of Laird Drive, south of Eglinton Avenue. Just after dinner on July 16, 1918, Lieutenant Tait and his mechanic decided to test out a biplane with a balky engine. Taking off, the plane had climbed about seventy-five feet when the engine quit. The craft plummeted earthward hitting the ground with a terrific crash and immediately burst into flames. Both the nineteen-year-old Tait and his mechanic were burned beyond recognition. The young flyer's memorial stone reads "KILLED AT LEASIDE AIRDROME". The Leaside airfield remained operational until 1931.

# Salvation Army's *Empress of Ireland* Monument

#4, plot R, lot 21

*E*arly in the morning of May 29, 1914, the Canadian Pacific ocean liner *Empress of Ireland* was struck by a Norwegian coal boat and in less than fifteen minutes the huge vessel disappeared beneath the cold waters of the St.Lawrence River. Aboard the *Empress* were 1,477 passengers and crew. When the final death toll was calculated, only 450 had survived the disaster. Of the 1,027 who had died 840 were passengers, 33 more than the number of passengers who had perished on the ill-fated Titanic a little more than twenty-five months earlier.

On board the *Empress* when she sailed from Quebec City on May 28, were 192 Salvation Army personnel on their way to the Army's World Congress in London, England. Of those, 167 Salvationists would never get there. In addition to the Salvationists from Toronto who were lost, an additional twenty-four Torontonians also drowned.

The few Salvation Army victims that were found after the disaster were returned to Toronto and a moving service was held in the old Mutual Street Arena on June 6. Following the service, a massive funeral cortege wound its way through crowd-lined streets to Mount Pleasant Cemetery, where sixteen victims were interred in the Salvation Army plot. Over the following weeks, the bodies of another six Salvation Army victims were found and buried in the plot for a total of twenty-two. In 1916, an impressive monument designed by Salvation Army Major Gideon Miller and sculpted by Emanuel Hahn was unveiled. Since the disaster, the Army has held an annual service of remembrance on the Sunday closest to May 29.

The Salvation Army has five plots in Mount Pleasant with 750 Salvationists interred there. The first recorded burial in a Salvation Army plot occurred on May 26, 1885.

MOUNT PLEASANT
CEMETERY

# James Bain, Jr.

#5, plot R, lot 32

*J*ames Bain Jr. was born in London, England on August 2, 1842, and came to Canada with his parents while still a child. He was educated in Toronto and then entered his father's stationery business. As the years went by, Bain worked for several other stationery firms, establishing a London, England office for one of them.

In 1882, he became Manager of the Canadian Publishing Company, a position he left the following year to accept the position of Chief Librarian for the newly established Toronto Public Library which opened to the public in the old Mechanic's Institute building at the northeast corner of Church and Adelaide Streets on March 10, 1884. Bain remained Chief Librarian until his death, caused by liver disease, on May 22, 1908. Interestingly, James Bain Jr. survived his father, James Bain Sr. by a mere four days. Bain Avenue in east-central Toronto is named for this prominent family.

# William Davies

#6, plot R, lot 40

**W**illiam Davies was born in the beautiful little town of Wallingford-on-Thames, Berkshire, England on June 23, 1831. After working in his father's provisions business for a few years, young William Davies set out for Canada in 1854. Davies has the distinction of being the country's first meat packer. His first job in the "new world" however, was on a farm at Little York, a few miles east of the bustling City of Toronto. He soon opened a stall in the South St. Lawrence Market and, with the successes gleaned from the exporting of cured hams and bacon, cheese, butter and lard to England, was able to establish his own large meat processing plant on Front Street at the corner of George in the early 1860s. This was the first building in Canada devoted to the curing and smoking of meats. Davies owed much of his success to his company's decision to supply the British markets with a more acceptable type of bacon than that supplied by American meat packers. It's quite likely that owing to the incredibly high volume of hogs processed in Davies' Toronto plant, the sobriquet "hogtown" became synonymous with our city.

In 1879, a new and larger plant was opened on Front Street adjacent to the Don River. During the winter months ice from the frozen river was cut and stored in an immense ice-house for year-round refrigeration purposes. In the early 1890s, the first artificial refrigeration equipment in the country was installed in the Front Street plant.

As Davies got older, he became totally deaf. This loss of hearing, combined with the fact that all but one of his offspring were to die before him,

**MOUNT PLEASANT CEMETERY**

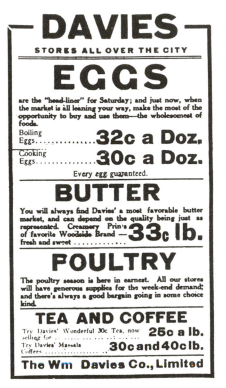

*Newspaper ad, 1914*

meant he'd have to look outside his immediate family for someone to take over operation of the company. Thus it was that in 1891, Joseph Flavelle (TRIANGLE 26) joined the company and a year later, the newly reorganized William Davies Company Limited was in place under the direct supervision of Flavelle.

In his declining years, Davies gave away much of his accumulated fortune. Since several of his sons had died from the effects of tuberculosis, Davies donated thousands of dollars to various charities that were fighting the ravages of that once dreaded disease. He also donated substantial sums of money to the Baptist Church and assorted schools and colleges.

It's ironic that while Davies spent virtually his entire life in the meat processing and packing business, it was a butt from a wayward goat Davies received while on holidays in one of the southern States that resulted in an injury that was to result in his death, just three months short of his ninetieth birthday. He died at his residence, 173 Warren Road, on March 21, 1921. On the day of the funeral, March 23, 1921, the William Davies Company processing plants and numerous retail stores were closed. The service was attended by hundreds who knew and respected the elderly gentleman.

# George Stewart Henry

#7, plot R, lot 41

*B*orn in King Township on July 17, 1871, Henry attended public school in Toronto, as well as the old Upper Canada College when it was on King Street, just across the street from today's Roy Thomson Hall. After graduation from Upper Canada College, Henry went to the University of Toronto, then on to the Ontario Agricultural College. With his interests in Holstein cattle, he was one of the founders of Farmers' Dairy and later, a director of Acme Farmers Dairy. Politically, Henry was on the York County Council from 1903 to 1910 and Reeve of York, 1907 to 1910. He also sat on the boards of the Toronto and York Roads Commission and the Niagara Parks Commission.

In 1913, Henry tried his hand at provincial politics, being elected M.P.P. for East York that year. Over the next two decades he held numerous important positions, including Minister of Agricul-

61

ture and Minister of Public Works and Highways. With the resignation of Premier Ferguson (PLOT 4, LOT 1) in late 1930, Henry was appointed Premier of the Province of Ontario, a post he held until his resignation in July, 1934. While Premier, he also held the posts of Provincial Treasurer and Minister of Education. Henry remained M.P.P. for East York until 1943.

On his death on September 2, 1958, George Henry was living on the ancestral Henry Farm (now a housing development northeast of today's Highway 401-Leslie Street interchange) that had been settled by former Premier Henry's Irish ancestors led by his great-grandfather Henry Mulholland in 1806.

Also listed on the Henry memorial is the name Robert Henry. He was George S. Henry's father who was drowned in the cold waters of Lake Superior escaping the steamer *Manitoulin* that caught fire early in the morning of May 18, 1882. In total, some twenty-five people were killed in that tragedy. The future tenth Premier of Ontario was five at the time.

# Nelson Davis

**# 8, plot S, lot 268**

*B*orn in Shaker Heights, a suburb of Cleveland, Ohio, Nelson Davis attended Cornell University, venturing into Canada in 1929, where over the next half century he made an incredible impact on this country's business community. Little was recorded about the man in the decades following his arrival in Canada.

He became better known in 1978, however, when he was made President, then Chairman of the extremely influential Argus Corporation. At the same time, he was also directly involved with nearly fifty other companies. For a time, Davis lived at Graydon Hall on Don Mills Road, which had been built by multi-millionaire Rupert Bain in 1936.

At the time of his death, Davis commuted between four residences, a summer home in Muskoka, a Toronto mansion overlooking the posh Rosedale golf course (when told one day he'd have to wait an hour to tee off, Davis built his own eighteen-hole course near Markham, Ontario) and two homes in Phoenix, Arizona. It was at one of the Phoenix houses that Davis accidentally drowned in the backyard swimming pool on March 13, 1979. He was seventy-three. He was buried following a private invitation only funeral service at St.John's Anglican Church, York Mills the following Saturday.

# Barry Britnell
### #9, plot I, lot 198

*B*arry's grandfather, Albert Britnell, emigrated to Toronto from Yorkshire, England and in 1893 opened a bookstore on lower Yonge Street. The business was eventually taken over by Albert's son Roy. In 1956, a third generation entered the busi-

**MOUNT PLEASANT CEMETERY**

ness when twenty-year-old Barry left his studies at the University of Toronto and joined his father in the running of the store. Barry Britnell, only forty-four years of age, died of cancer on October 1, 1980. Today, the Albert Britnell Book Shop, now managed by Barry's widow Mary Ellen, remains as one of the country's best and most respected book stores.

 # Joseph Simpson
## #10, plot H, lot 45

*B*orn in Charlestown (Charleston), South Carolina in 1823 and educated in one of the local private schools, young Simpson entered the business world at the age of thirteen as a clerk in one of that southern city's dry goods stores. In 1848, he was one of the thousands who rushed west to earn fame and fortune in the gold fields of California. There, in addition to being a miner, Simpson also ran a hotel. With the outbreak of the war between the States in 1863, Simpson decided to emigrate to Canada where he obtained work in the grain business. Less than a year later, he began manufacturing knitted goods which eventually led him to establish the Toronto Knitting Company. The enterprise grew to become one of the largest knitting and yarn companies in the country. The Toronto Knitting Company's factory on lower Berkeley Street has recently been restored and is now called Berkeley Castle. Joseph Simpson died on August 7, 1898. A total of nine members of the Simpson family are interred in the family mausoleum.

# Stephen
# Alexander Oliver
## #11, plot H, lot 46, private

*T*his is another "mystery man" in Mount Pleasant Cemetery. All we know about Stephen Oliver is that he and a J. B. Ryan were partners in Ryan and Oliver Company, importers of hardware and tools, 114 Yonge Street. City directories indicate the company was in business for several decades. Oliver lived at 25 Brock Street, now part of Spadina Avenue south of King Street. He died on August 1, 1881 at the age of forty-nine. The Oliver mausoleum was built following his death. Also in the mausoleum are Frances (d.1878), Ellen (d.1892), Mary Ann (d.1893) and Stephen Jr.(d.1905). It is assumed the first lady is Stephen Alexander's wife, while the last three are their children.

# Jeremiah Carty
## #12, plot H, lot 49, 50

*A* total of six members of the Carty family are interred in this stately mausoleum. On June 28, 1883, Jeremiah Carty and his wife Mary were removed from the Necropolis, where they had been buried following their deaths on September 8, 1868 and May 27, 1876, respectively, and rein-

terred in the newly constructed family mausoleum. Both had been buried in the Necropolis, as they had died before Mount Pleasant Cemetery opened. On October 31, 1927 and January 6, 1933, daughters Mary and Martha were also interred in the family mausoleum. Unfortunately, little is recorded about the Carty family, other than Jeremiah arrived in Toronto (then York) from Ireland in 1830 when he was ten years of age. The 1860-61 city directory reveals Jeremiah operated a soap and candle factory at Queen and George Streets in a plant he had built in 1845. He was also an Alderman representing St. David's Ward during the period 1858-1860. Carty was also one of the founders and Vice-President of the Western Canada Savings and Loan Company. These rather specific items are tempered somewhat by information in the 1874 directory that indicates that Mary is now a widow - two full years before cemetery burial records indicate her husband actually passed away! Two other Carty family members, George and Emma Carty, are also in the vault having been removed from St. James' Cemetery where they were originally interred on August 23, 1853 and September 6, 1857.

# John Fulton

#13, plot H, sec lot 53

*L*ittle is known about Fulton's early life. We do know from his brief obituary in the Evening Telegram newspaper that he became a well respected local physician and was editor of the prestigious Canadian Lancet magazine for fifteen years. Dr.

Fulton was a professor of surgery at the old Trinity Medical School and practiced at the Toronto General Hospital on Gerrard Street East. In the early spring of 1887, the good doctor contracted a cold which developed into pneumonia which in turn was aggravated by typhoid fever. Dr. John Fulton passed away at his residence at 303 Church Street on May 15, 1887.

# Guy Simmonds
## #14, plot H, lot 573

*B*orn in Surrey, England in April, 1903, Simmonds came to Canada with his parents when he was nine-years-old. In 1925, he graduated from Royal Military College, first in his class. During the Second World War, Simmonds became Canada's youngest General and led the 2nd Canadian Corps drive through northwestern Europe. On May 5, 1945, the 1st Canadian Army under Simmond's command marched into Holland where the unconditional surrender of the German forces was accepted. Called the "liberator of Holland", Simmonds was also described by Field Marshal Viscount Montgomery as "the best product of the Allied side". Following the end of hostilities, Simmonds took command of the Canadian Defence College and the Staff College. He was then appointed Chief of the General Staff and became Colonel-in-Chief of the Toronto-based Royal Regiment of Canada.

In the business world, Simmonds was President of United Ceramics, Frontenac Floor and Tile and the Toronto Brick Company. He was also Vice-

President and a Director of Commercial Life and Halifax Insurance. Following a long illness, General Guy Simmonds C.C., C.B., C.B.E., D.S.O. died on May 15, 1974. Three days later, a funeral service was held at Grace Church-on-the-Hill followed by a procession during which the body was borne to Mount Pleasant Cemetery on a flag-draped gun carriage. At the cemetery, there was a full military burial service, complete with rifle salute.

 # James Maher
### #15, plot H, lot 513

*B*orn in Toronto, young Maher attended public and high school in Picton, Ontario. At the age of twenty-one, he established the Reliance Shoe Company in Toronto and nineteen years later opened a chain of retail stores throughout the province under the name Maher Shoe Stores. He also served on the Metro Toronto Planning Board for eight years and the City of Toronto Planning Board for another seventeen. During the Second World War, Maher's company sponsored the extremely popular "March of Toys" variety show on radio station CFRB, with all proceeds going to the British War Veterans' Fund.

# George Montegu Black

#16, plot H, lot 502

*G*raduating from the University of Manitoba in 1933 at the age of twenty-two, Black became a chartered accountant in 1937 and two years later was appointed Comptroller of Western Breweries Limited. With the outbreak of war, he joined the R.C.A.F. and was transferred to a civilian post in the Department of National Defence for Air where he was one of a group that helped initiate the highly successful British Commonwealth Air Training Plan, referred to by U.S. President Roosevelt as the "aerodrome of democracy".

Following the end of the war, Black joined Canadian Breweries becoming President of the company in 1950, a position he held until his retirement eight years later. George Montegu Black, father of Conrad and G. Montegu III, died on June 29, 1976, just ten days after the death of his wife, who is also buried in this plot.

 # Argero Stratas

#17, plot S, lot 201

*B*orn on the Island of Crete, the former Argero Terezakis emigrated to Canada when still a young

woman and lived with her brothers in Toronto. In 1928, she married Emanuel Stratakis and ten years later, while the couple were living at 276A George Street in the Dundas-Jarvis Street neighbourhood, a daughter was born. Today, we know their daughter better as internationally acclaimed soprano and former Metropolitan Opera star Teresa Stratas.

Argero died on September 10, 1963, at the age of fifty-three. Teresa's father Emanuel was eighty-three when he passed away on June 15, 1987. He is also buried in the Stratas plot in Mount Pleasant Cemetery.

 # Edmund Burke

#18, plot 12, lot 20

*B*orn in Ireland, Edmund Burke emigrated to Toronto with his family where he attended Jesse Ketchum School and Upper Canada College. He then entered the architectural firm of Gundy and Langley as a student. From 1872 until 1892, he was in partnership with Mr. Langley, his uncle, subsequently assuming the business of the recently deceased William Storm.

A few of the buildings designed by Burke that are still standing include Old St. Andrew's Church, Jarvis and Carlton Streets (1878); Sherbourne Street Methodist Church (now St. Luke's United); Sherbourne and Carlton Streets (remodeled 1886); Trinity Methodist (now United) Church, Bloor Street West (1889); Walmer Road Baptist Church (1892) and the Robert Simpson Building, at the southwest corner of Yonge and Queen Streets (both

*Queen Street looking west across Yonge, c.1906. The Burke-designed Simpson store on the left.*

the 1893 structure, which was destroyed by fire and the new store, which replaced the fire-ravaged building in 1895). Burke was also consulting architect on the Prince Edward Viaduct that connects Bloor Street with the Danforth.

At the time of his death on January 2, 1919, Burke was head of the firm Burke, Horwood and White. He succumbed to complications brought on by pneumonia and passed away in his residence at 23 South Drive in Rosedale.

# James Fluke

#19, plot Q, lot 20

*U*nfortunately, little is known about this gentleman other than that he was a steamboat captain

who had settled in Blackstock, Ontario and operated a mill and a hotel called the Australia House. He eventually made his way to Toronto and is found in the city directories living on King Street near Spadina Avenue in the latter part of the last century. He died on April 12, 1894 at the age of seventy and was originally buried in Plot C. He was moved to the "Captain Fluke" mausoleum when his wife (who had obviously remarried after the captain's death), Charlotte Fluke Staples, died on October 27, 1920. It is assumed she had the mausoleum built in Fluke's memory. It is not unusual to find a floral memorial at the door to the mausoleum, but who places it there is a mystery.

# Forsey Page
## # 20, plot Q, lot 22

*T*oronto-born Forsey Page attended Harbord Collegiate, St. Andrew's College and the University of Toronto, graduating with a degree in architecture. After a year of travel in England and France, he returned to Toronto and started his career in the employ of a local architectural firm. In 1925, he formed a partnership with Harland Steele and together the team designed such diverse city landmarks as the former College of Pharmacy on Gerrard Street East, St. Clements Church in North Toronto, the award-winning Garden Court residential development on Bayview Avenue, the Toronto Board of Education's Education Centre on College Street, the C.N.E.'s Queen Elizabeth Building, the O'Keefe Centre, and the Procter and Gamble Building at the northwest corner of St. Clair Avenue and Yonge Street. Page won many personal awards and was a Fellow of the Royal Institute of British Architects and a Senator of the University of Toronto. Forsey Page died on November 22, 1970 at the age of eighty-five.

# John Davis

## # 21, plot Q, lot 26

*N*ow just a city street and a station on Metro Toronto's first subway line, Davisville was for many years a thriving community well north of the city limits. It was named for John Davis who arrived in Canada from his native England in 1840.

His first job was as a bookkeeper in Toronto, a position he gave up five years later to venture out into the countryside north of the city and start a pottery business called John Davis and Son. Also known as the Davisville Pottery Works, the business turned out earthenware manufactured in the plant that stood on the east side of Yonge, just north of the present Davisville Avenue. It was the

MOUNT PLEASANT
CEMETERY

community of Davisville's only industry. The clay was obtained from pits east of the plant and near today's Eglinton Avenue East extension through the Don Valley.

The pottery plant moved to 377 Merton Street in the early 1900s and moved again to 607 Merton Street (now Pottery Playgrounds) in 1916, both locations backing onto Mount Pleasant Cemetery. The company turned out clay products for a total of eighty-five years.

John Davis died on April 29, 1891, and is buried in the Davis family plot along with his wife Mary (d.1889) and the couple's seven children, the most recent to pass away being Joseph Stanley Davis who died September 9, 1951, just ten weeks before his one-hundredth birthday.

 # Masonic Monument

## # 22, plot Q, lot 60

*John Ross Robertson, who donated Masonic plot*

*T*he large burial plot surrounding the striking Masonic monument was given to the Masonic Order in 1883 by one of its most celebrated members, John Ross Robertson, founder of the *Evening Telegram* newspaper and himself a staunch member of the Craft. The first burial in this plot occurred that same year. The monument, which had been designed by F. B. Gullett, another member of the Craft, was unveiled by Robertson, a past Grand Master on June 24, 1893. The ritual took place following a parade of 800 Masons from the Masonic Temple on Toronto Street through city streets to the cemetery. This is still an active burial plot.

# Allen Neilson

## # 23, plot Q, lot 407

*T*he William Neilson Company was established on Gladstone Avenue in west-central Toronto by William Neilson in 1893. Following William's death in 1915, his eldest son Morden became President. In 1948, following Morden's death, the company was sold to the George Weston Company and Charles Neilson, William's second eldest son, took over the presidency. After Charles' death in 1951, William's youngest boy Allen became President. This accounts for the familiar Neilson corporate script appearing on the memorial stone. Allen Neilson died on September 3, 1971.

# Constantine Boukydis

#24, plot Q, lot 402

*B*orn in Sparta, Greece, Gus Boukydis emigrated to Chicago in 1900, and began peddling fruit and vegetables from a small pushcart. Gus and his brothers eventually moved to London, Ontario, then on to Toronto where in 1912 they went into the candy-making business. Soon Gus opened a restaurant at 181 Yonge Street and, remembering the statue of Diana, goddess of the hunt prominently on display in the town square back in Sparta, called his establishment Diana Sweets. At one time there were four Diana Sweets restaurants in Metropolitan Toronto, and the founder kept a close eye on all of them until he retired in 1960 from the business he started many years before. Gus Boukydis died on October 2, 1969.

# Arthur William Miles

#25, plot Q, lot 180

$B$orn in Toronto in 1873, Miles obtained his first job at the age of nine as a page boy at the old Parliament Buildings on Front Street West, just west of Simcoe Street. After a brief stint as a miner in South Africa, he returned to Toronto and entered the undertaking business at the turn-of-the-century, with a small funeral parlour on College Street near Spadina Avenue. In 1920, he moved the business to St. Clair Avenue, just west of Yonge Street, where it remained until the business was acquired by the Humphrey funeral people. They closed the St. Clair building and made their Bayview Avenue parlour the A. W. Miles Chapel. One of the innovations Miles introduced to the funeral business was the motorized hearse. Many people frowned on such use of the new-fangled vehicles as they considered the speed of such vehicles disrespectful.

77

**MOUNT PLEASANT CEMETERY**

Back in 1912, Miles built a summer home at Mimico, Ontario and maintained a small zoo and picnic ground nearby. Twenty-four years later, the zoo was transferred to a two-hundred acre farm, north of the Dundas Highway in Erindale. There was never any admission charge to Miles' Zoo. In 1943, a major fire destroyed much of the zoo and stock. The attraction was soon rebuilt, but only lasted another dozen or so years. Arthur W. Miles died at his Erindale, Ontario home on June 18, 1956.

# Charles William Rayner

#26, plot Q, lot 250

*B*orn in Suffolk, England, Rayner came to Canada at the age of seven. He attended schools in Thorold and St. Catharines, Ontario, before entering an engineering course at the University of Toronto. The Rayner Construction Company's first job in Toronto was building the Bayview Avenue bridge over the Don River, just north of Lawrence Avenue, which he undertook in 1925. Other projects for Manitoba Hydro and Ontario Hydro followed, one of the largest being the $45 million project to build twin hydraulic diversion tunnels under the City of Niagara Falls, taking water from above the falls to new Sir Adam Beck Generating Station Number Two down river. Rayner Construction also built miles and miles of highways, an undetermined number of traffic bridges and a large portion of the St. Lawrence Seaway.

In his younger days, Rayner had also been a pioneer amongst the prospectors. In 1915-16, he surveyed and opened a quarry on the north shore of Georgian Bay for a small Buffalo, New York company that was eventually to become known as Union Carbide. Rayner Construction was also involved in the construction of the country's first subway, the T.T.C.'s Yonge line which opened on March 30, 1954. George William Rayner died on January 1, 1958 at the age of seventy-four.

# John Morison

## #27, plot Q, lot 10

*Residence of John Morison, Jarvis St.*

*M*orison was born in Alloa, Scotland in April, 1839. Following the death of his parents, he moved to Glasgow and then emigrated to Toronto in 1851.

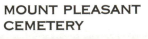

**MOUNT PLEASANT CEMETERY**

His first job in the provincial capital paid an annual salary of just five pounds ($25). Morison eventually entered the wholesale grocery business, starting his own company in 1864. Twenty years later he retired, a very wealthy man.

In addition to his grocery business, Morison was also Governor of the British America Assurance Company and a Director of the North American Life Assurance Company and Toronto, Grey and Bruce Railway. He also served one term, 1873, as City Alderman for St. James' Ward. John Morison died August 22, 1917 and is interred in the mausoleum along with seven other members of the Morison family, including his wife Sarah who died in 1911, the year their mausoleum was built.

#  J. Keiller MacKay

## #28, plot Q, lot 154

*B*orn in Plainfield, Nova Scotia on July 11, 1888, young MacKay was educated at Pictou Academy and St. Francis Xavier before the outbreak of war curtailed his studies. MacKay enlisted and was sent overseas with the 6th Brigade Canadian Field Artillery. He served with distinction before being seriously wounded by shrapnel at Vimy Ridge. A metal-backed notebook that he carried in his breast pocket saved his life.

Recovering in a Halifax hospital, the young man began to study law and was awarded his degree from Dalhousie University in 1922. He was then called to the bar of Nova Scotia and a year later to the bar of Ontario. He held several important judicial posts including Justice of the Supreme

Court of Ontario. In 1957, Prime Minister Diefenbaker appointed MacKay Ontario's nineteenth Lieutenant Governor, a post he held until his resignation in 1963. He then went on to become the first Chairman of the Ontario Council for the Arts. MacKay, who also held several important directorships, died at the Toronto General Hospital on June 12, 1970.

# Herbert A. Bruce

### # 29, plot Q, lot 143

*B*orn in 1868, the son of a poor pioneer farmer who worked the family farm near Lake Scugog, Ontario, Herbert Alexander Bruce attended high school in Port Perry, Ontario. He graduated from the Toronto School of Medicine, not yet integrated with the University of Toronto, in 1892. In 1912, Bruce established his seventy-two bed Wellesley Hospital in an old residence at the northwest corner of Wellesley and Sherbourne Streets. With the outbreak of war two years later, he was appointed Inspector-General of Medical Services overseas. Dr. Bruce managed to "ruffle a lot of feathers" (especially those of Canadian War Minister Sir Sam Hughes) and was summarily dismissed. Bruce was enlisted by the British War Office and assigned as consulting surgeon to its armies in France. He was also Professor Emeritus, Clinical Surgery, University of Toronto and Consulting Surgeon, Toronto General Hospital.

In 1932, Bruce was appointed Ontario's fifteenth Lieutenant Governor, a position he held

MOUNT PLEASANT
CEMETERY

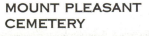

for five years. As such, his official residence was a beautiful mansion called Chorley Park in North Rosedale overlooking the Don Valley. Bruce was the last of five Lieutenant Governors to occupy the million dollar structure (it was originally budgeted in 1911 at $215,000), and, when his tenure ended, the building was closed as a cost cutting measure only to be reopened as a military hospital during the Second World War. In 1959, Chorley Park was demolished.

Dr. Bruce died of a heart attack, at the age of ninety-four, on Sunday, June 23, 1963 at his home, 18 Douglas Drive in Rosedale, a dwelling located within walking distance of the site of his former vice-regal residence that was once beautifully situated in a grassy realm now called Chorley Park.

# Robert Hood Saunders

*# 30, plot Q, lot 207*

*B*ob Saunders was born on May 30, 1903 in Toronto and educated in the local school system. He obtained his degree in law and was called to the bar in 1927. Eight years later, Saunders tried his hand at municipal politics and was successful, being elected Alderman for Ward Four in 1935 to 1940 (except 1938 and 1939) and Controller from 1941 to 1944. In 1945 municipal elections, he defeated the incumbent, becoming the city's chief magistrate. Saunders was Mayor until February of 1948, when he resigned to become the Chairman of Ontario Hydro. Although he had no formal training in any of the engineering disciplines, it was Saunders who was responsible in great measure for Ontario Hydro's Niagara River power developments at Queenston and for instigating a long

  **MOUNT PLEASANT CEMETERY**

sought after start on the massive St. Lawrence Seaway and Power project. It was while travelling on Ontario Hydro business that Saunders was killed when the ice-encrusted Grumman *Mallard* aircraft in which he was a passenger crashed while approaching the London, Ontario airport. The accident occurred early in the morning of January 15, 1955. Fifty-one-year-old Robert Hood Saunders succumbed to his injuries the following day.

# Henry Northrop/ George H. Gooderham

## # 31, plot T, lot 3

*B*orn in New York State in 1821, Henry Northrop joined with fellow American John Lyman to form the Northrop and Lyman Company that specialized in the manufacture and sale of various patent medicines. In 1854, the company moved to New-castle, Ontario and twenty years later re-established itself again, this time in the bustling City of Toronto, with an office and warehouse at 21 Front Street West. When Henry Northrop died on November 20, 1893, he was interred in the cemetery's vault until the fortress-like family mausoleum was completed in the fall of the follow-ing year. Henry's wife Mary (d.1899) is also interred in the Northrop mausoleum.

George Horace Gooderham, a member of the city's prominent Gooderham family, and husband of the former Cora Northrop, is also buried in the

84

*George Horace
Gooderham*

mausoleum. Gooderham, the grandson of William
Gooderham who, with James Worts, established the
Gooderham and Worts distilling empire in 1832,
was born in Toronto on April 18, 1868. Educated
at the Normal School and the old Jarvis Collegiate
Institute, Gooderham was always keenly interested
in the city's educational system, an interest that
prompted him to run for and win the position of
School Trustee. He remained a Trustee from 1890
until 1903 and in 1904 was elected School Board
Chairman, a post he held for another four years.
In 1908, Gooderham was elected M.P.P. for the
riding of Toronto South, being re-elected in 1911
and 1914. He was also President of the Canadian
National Exhibition from 1908 until 1910, President of Ridley College and a director of several
financial institutions. Gooderham had a passion for
yachting and held the position of Commodore of
the Royal Canadian Yacht Club for more than a
decade. He skippered his many yachts, which
included the famous *Oriole III*, *Oriole IV* and
*Cleopatra* to many national and international

championships. George Horace Gooderham died at his residence, 204 St.George Street, on December 22, 1942. His wife Cora (d.1962) is also buried in the Northrop-Gooderham mausoleum.

# James French

## # 32, plot T, lot 4

A glass blower by profession, James French came to Toronto in 1836, from New York City at the age of nineteen. In the young Canadian city, he took up a number of different jobs including that of a fruit vendor, meat packer and real estate agent. For a time, French owned and managed the old Royal Lyceum theatre on King Street West that stood where the Toronto-Dominion Centre now stands. The playhouse, which was erected in 1848 and was one of the city's first legitimate venues, was destroyed by fire while under the ownership of James French. Adequately covered by insurance, French was probably lucky that the place burned as the newly constructed Grand Opera House on nearby Adelaide Street would otherwise have shortly put him and his theatre out of business. James French died on May 22, 1892 at his residence, 123 Yorkville Avenue, and was originally interred in the Necropolis. He was removed to his new mausoleum two years later. James French rests alone in this magnificent structure. Mrs. French remarried soon after her husband's death and is buried with her second husband. Other family members are buried in the family plot above and behind the mausoleum.

# George Dennis Morse

## # 33, plot T, lot 6

**B**orn in Cleveland, Ohio in 1833, George Morse came to Toronto with his family in 1836. Educated in Toronto, George and his two brothers, John and William, began a feeding and cattle shipping business in 1864. Most of the livestock were destined for foreign markets. Nine years later, George Morse established G. D. Morse and Company Soap and Candle Works with an office on West Market Street and a large, three-acre factory on Front Street near the Don River. The company produced huge quantities of both laundry and toilet soaps that were shipped to all parts of the Dominion. In addition to soap, the company was a major producer of tallow candles. Morse retired from the soap business in 1877 and devoted all his time to the cattle business which by then had become one of the largest in the province.

Morse met an untimely end on June 27, 1887, while returning from his extensive complex of cattle barns that were located adjacent to the Gooderham and Worts distillery complex on the waterfront, east of Parliament Street. For many years large herds of cattle were kept near the distillery, so they could be fed the inexpensive mash by-product that resulted from the distilling process. Late in the evening, as Morse returned to the city along the railway tracks that paralleled Toronto Harbour, he attempted to get out of the way of an approaching train, slipped down the embankment, hit his head and fell into the bay and drowned.

George D. Morse and six family members are interred in the Morse vault.

# Theodore Heintzman

#34, plot T, lot 10

*B*orn in Berlin, Germany on May 19, 1817, Theodore Heintzman (no relation to Gerhard Heintzman
PLOT 1, LOT 13) was in the piano manufacturing
business before he emigrated with his family to
the United States in 1850. He spent some time in
the same business in both New York City and
Buffalo, New York. With the outbreak of the
American Civil War, the demand for pianos fell
drastically and Heintzman decided to move to
Toronto, where he and the family rented a house
on Duke (Adelaide) Street. In a back room of the
little house, Heintzman began manufacturing
pianos that for the first time bore his own name.
The business flourished and soon the house was
too small for the family and the factory. Heintzman moved his piano business into a large factory
on King Street West, which he also outgrew. In
1891, Heintzman eventually built a brand new
complex out in the Town of West Toronto Junction
where the Heintzman piano was manufactured for
a great many years. On July 25, 1899, after a long
illness, eighty-two-year-old Theodore Heintzman
died at his beautiful Annette Street residence.

# Independent Order of Oddfellows Memorial

### #35, plot T, lot ONE

*E*rected at a cost of $2,000, the unique I.O.O.F. memorial was designed by Herbert G. Paull with the work carried out by Fred B. Gullett and Sons, sculptors at their studio located at 740-742 Yonge Street. It is made out of Bedford, Indiana limestone with columns made of granite from New Brunswick. The memorial stands twenty-seven feet high, the globe at the pinnacle measures two-and-a-half feet in diameter and incorporated into the work are some twenty symbols emblematic of the I.O.O.F. The memorial was unveiled with fitting ceremonies on October 30, 1897. Many members of the I.O.O.F. are interred in the ground surrounding the memorial. This is still an active burial plot.

# St. Andrew's Society Monument

### #36, plot U, lot ONE

*W*hile 1836 is considered as the founding date for the St. Andrew's Society in Toronto, early community newspapers indicate that Scotsmen got together to celebrate St. Andrew's Day as early as

89

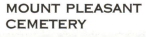

1822. To be completely accurate, however, this benevolent society was formed on May 5, 1836, with William Allan as the organization's first President. In November of 1886, the society purchased a large burial plot in Mount Pleasant Cemetery. Several years later, a handsome monument was erected and dedicated on June 20, 1891 by the society's President Dr. Daniel Clark. The first burial in the St. Andrew's plot was on May 5, 1886, when James Tulloch was laid to rest. This is still an active burial plot.

# John Anderson Carlaw

**# 37, plot U, lot 25**

*A* native of Stirling, Scotland, Carlaw came to Canada in 1853 with his father, who was manager of a large Scottish syndicate that was involved with the development of the Quebec Division of the Grand Trunk Railway. The younger Carlaw joined the railway in 1857 and was appointed cashier of the company in Toronto, six years later. He remained in the employ of the Grand Trunk for over thirty years, eventually retiring to devote himself to the administration of his extensive land holdings. One property was adjacent to that of George Leslie in the east end of Toronto. When Carlaw subdivided the property, he ran a north-south thoroughfare through the middle giving, it his surname.

In 1861, and with the sanction of the Government, the railway recruited its own military force to help defend its extensive holdings against any possible insurrection. The unit formed in the City of Toronto had Mr. Carlaw as Captain of Number 1 Toronto Company. For many years they mustered in their own drill shed on Wellington Street, just west of Simcoe. In 1866 and again in 1870, when the Fenian disturbance threatened along the Niagara River, the Grand Trunk units were ready to go, but as hostilities subsided the fellows went back to their everyday jobs. Captain Carlaw eventually took over command of the Toronto battalion and was elevated to the rank of Major, a position he held until all the units were disbanded in the mid-1870s.

John A. Carlaw died at Rosebank, his residence at 404 Avenue Road, on October 15, 1923 at

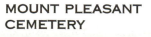

the age of eighty-three. Also interred in the family plot is John Clarke Carlaw, John Anderson Carlaw's twenty-three-year-old son, who drowned while bathing in Lake Ontario at the foot of Dunn Avenue on August 8, 1901.

# Mark Bredin
## #38, plot C, sec 13, lot 21

*B*orn in Dublin, Ireland on July 2, 1863, Mark Bredin emigrated to Toronto in 1883. Within weeks, the twenty-year-old embarked on a career in bread making and soon Bredin and his brother opened their own small bakery on Yonge Street. In 1902, the Bredin boys opened a new, ultra-modern plant on the west side of Avenue Road just north of Dupont Street. The Bredin Bread Company soon became one of the largest bakeries in the city.

Nine years later, Mark Bredin and three other bakers, including forty-six-year-old George Weston (PLOT 19, LOT 27), joined with multi-millionaire stockbroker Cawthra Mulock and together they established the Canada Bread Company, Limited.

Young Mulock, who had recently spent $750,000 on the construction of his new Royal Alexandra Theatre on King Street West, served as the company's first president, a position assumed a few years later by Bredin. The latter served as President and General Manager of Canada Bread until 1929 when he retired, subsequently re-establishing the Bredin Bread Company, this time at 559 Davenport Road.

Mark Bredin died at the Toronto General Hospital at the age of seventy-two on October 19, 1935. He was interred two days later.

Canada Bread went on to become one of the largest bakeries in the county. Since 1969, it has operated under the name Corporate Foods Limited.

# John Charles Henry Copp

### # 39, plot U, lot 26

*J*ohnny Copp, as he was known to his myriad of friends, was born in Toronto on September 26, 1911. On December 3, 1933 the popular University of Toronto football star was dead, gunned down in the prime of life. His murderer has never been found.

On the evening of Thursday, November 30, 1933 Johnny and his friend Edmund Houston had been studying in a room on the third floor of the Copp residence at 96 Wellesley Street East. That evening, Johnny's mother was hosting a bridge party and most of the guests were busy down on the main floor playing their respective hands. As Johnny made his way to the second floor to use the telephone, through the landing window he saw someone outside on the porch roof skulking in the shadows. Yelling to Houston that someone was try- ing to break in, presumably to rifle the pockets of the guests' clothes thrown across the beds on the

second floor, Johnny rushed down the stairs, out the back door and confronted the person now purposely hidden in the shadows where the porch roof joined the house. A shot rang out.

The burglar fled over the back fence and a stricken Johnny Copp staggered up the back porch steps, into the house and collapsed on the kitchen floor. The police and an ambulance were called and the young man was soon in the operating room of the Wellesley Hospital where for three hours medical experts, including Dr. Herbert Bruce and the boys own father Dr. Charles Copp, himself a prominent Toronto surgeon, worked to stop the bleeding. It looked for a while as if the twenty-two-year-old would make it, but after numerous transfusions using blood donated by many of Johnny's football and fraternity friends, the young man died the following Sunday.

So great was the grief exhibited by his fellow students, family friends and ordinary Torontonians, it was decided by the university President Dr. Henry Cody that classes would be cancelled on

Tuesday, December 5 and a public funeral held in Convocation Hall on the university grounds. This was the first time that someone other than a university official or political figure had been accorded such an honour.

Notables at the funeral and in the procession from Convocation Hall to Mt. Pleasant Cemetery included Mayor William Stewart and a large number of city council members, provincial and federal government and university officials, plus thousands of grieving citizens. Though dozens of suspects were rounded up and questioned over the ensuing years, no one was ever charged with Johnny's murder. Many things may have changed since 1933, but Johnny's church still maintains a special room named in memory of the young man. And to this day, the University of Toronto continues to award both a football trophy and scholarship in the name of Johnny Copp.

# John Beaty
## # 40, plot U, lot C

*T*he third person to settle in the area west of Dufferin Street when it was still "out in the country" was John Beaty. He was born in Ireland in 1825 and emigrated to Toronto in 1845. His first employment was assisting his uncle James collect tolls on the roads along the lakeshore leading to and from the little town. In 1859, the young man married Jeanette Triller (Triller Avenue in Parkdale is named for her family) and in 1871 was appointed to Her Majesty's Customs Service. A year later, in one of the great Toronto real estate

**MOUNT PLEASANT CEMETERY**

deals of all time, he purchased the large estate of Colonel Dunn of the 100th Regiment that stretched from today's Dowling Avenue west to Roncesvalles for $200 an acre.

He spent the rest of his life in comfort, selling off parcels of land as the Town of Parkdale grew, eventually becoming part of the city in 1889. Beaty Avenue is named for this gentleman who died at his residence, 1499 Queen Street West, on November 10, 1908.

# Herbert Laurence Rous

## #41, plot U, lot 208

*B*orn on September 9, 1879, in Belleville, Ontario, Rous attended the local public and high school, leaving before graduation so he could embark on a printing career. He joined the Belleville Intelligencer newspaper which was owned by Mackenzie Bowell who later became Canada's fifth Prime Minister. After five years in the newspaper business, Rous came to Toronto where he was employed by several printers before joining the Southam Press. Here he met Frederick Mann and in 1909 the two struck out on their own, establishing Rous and Mann Limited (later Rous and Mann Press Limited). The partners new printing company was the first in Canada to establish and maintain a full-time art department, employing such internationally famous artists as Tom Thomson, Stanley Turner, F. H. Varley, Frank Carmichael and Alfred Casson, the latter three best-known as members of Canada's Group of Seven. The Rous and Mann Press Limited soon became one of the most respected quality printing houses in the country.

During the First World War, Rous served as a Captain with the Canadian Expeditionary Forces overseas. He was also a Director and President of the Ontario College of Art, the Poppy Fund of Toronto and a Trustee of the Toronto General Burial Grounds (now Toronto Trust Cemeteries) from 1944 until his death on December 1, 1964.

# Edward Samuel Rogers

### #42, plot U, lot 120

*Young Ted Rogers had a passion for wireless telephony.*

*B*orn on June 21, 1900 and educated in the University of Toronto Schools, Rogers was fascinated with wireless telephony. He and his brother

Elsworth could frequently be found experimenting with the newest wonder of the age in the living room of their home at 49 Nanton Avenue in Toronto's posh Rosedale. After finishing U.T.S., Ted went on to the University of Toronto where he graduated with a degree in engineering. In 1922, he joined the Independent Telephone Company. For the next two years, the company's well-stocked lab became the young inventor's home away from home.

During a visit to a radio laboratory in the United States, Rogers met an inventor who had perfected the alternating current radio tube. The young Torontonian saw the possibility of creating a "batteryless radio" using the American's new tube in conjunction with special circuitry that Rogers himself would design. After purchasing the Canadian rights for the tube, he returned to Toronto and in 1924 started his own company which he called the Standard Radio Manufacturing Corporation. Later, after agreeing to sell the American-made Majestic model, it became the Rogers-Majestic Corporation. The next year, 1925, Rogers put the world's first alternating current radio on the market. Now radio listeners could forego the costly and cumbersome batteries that had been necessary to power the older sets. For $260, plus $45 for a speaker, they could purchase one of Ted Rogers' "batteryless" models and simply plug it into the wall. The next logical step for the young man was to start his own radio station, where he could air programs that would give people a reason to purchase radios. The twenty-seven-year-old transformed his amateur radio station 3BP into CFRB (the letters RB for Rogers Batteryless) that went on the air for the first time on February 19, 1927 from the second floor of Tommy Ryans' Jarvis Street art gallery. With a future as bright as the tuning eye on his "batteryless" radio, Edward Samuel Rogers passed away at the all-too-young age of thirty-eight on May 6, 1939.

# William Griffith Trethewey

### # 43, plot U, lot 39

**B**orn in the Muskoka area of Ontario in 1867, Trethewey spent much of his early life in British Columbia where he engaged in prospecting. In 1906, he returned to his native province and began prospecting in the Cobalt area of northern Ontario where he made a major silver discovery. He subsequently sold both the Trethewey Mine, as it became known, and his interest in the Conlagas Mine for over one million dollars. In 1913, Trethewey moved to England where he acquired a large residence called Holmstead Place in Sussex where hundreds of Canadian troops were entertained during the First World War.

Following the end of hostilities, Trethewey returned to Toronto and took up residence on a 600-acre farm near Weston in York Township. It was at this farm in 1910 that several early aviation meets were held. In fact, the first airplane to fly over the City of Toronto took off from and returned to the grass covered airfield on what became the Trethewey farm. In the mid-1920s, 400-acres of the farm were subdivided into factory lots and the owner spent $60,000 to build a road diagonally through the property connecting Jane Street with Eglinton Avenue near the Keele Street intersection. Called Holmstead Drive, Trethewey dedicated his new thoroughfare to the Townships of North York and York. Following his death, the street was renamed Trethewey Drive. Trethewey also had plans to turn the remaining 200-acres into a modern planned community. However, while wintering in Sarasota, Florida, William Griffith

Trethewey died on March 6, 1926. His remains were returned to Toronto for burial which occurred one week later.

 # Stephen B. Chandler

## # 44, plot U, lot 59

*T*his is another Toronto businessman about whom little is known. The city directories of the era show he owned a surgical and dental supply company located at 110 Victoria Street and resided at 79 Spencer Avenue in Parkdale. He died at the age of seventy-one on October 28, 1898, buried in PLOT U, LOT 48 and re-interred in this impressive mausoleum on June 5, 1901, soon after its completion. With the most recent interment in 1979, a total of eleven people now rest in the Chandler mausoleum.

 # Walter Sutherland Lee

## # 45, plot U, lot 58

*A* native of the City of Toronto, where he was born on October 18, 1837, Lee was educated at Mair's Private Academy, after which he started his business career as a bookkeeper with Consumers' Gas. He then became Managing Director of the

Western Canada Loan Company and a few years later General Manager of Canada Permanent Mortgage Corporation. He was also a director of several prominent companies. In addition to his business responsibilities, Lee was extremely civic minded being a School Board Trustee (later Chairman) for thirty-five years, on the Board (later Chairman) of the Toronto General Hospital for twenty-five years, a long-time member of the Mechanics' Institute and a founding member of the Toronto Industrial Exhibition Board (after 1912, the Board of the Canadian National Exhibition). Lee owned a large plot of land in the Beach area of Toronto. Lee Avenue is named for him while Leuty Avenue is named for his wife, the former Emma Mary Leuty. Walter S. Lee died at his residence, 306 Jarvis Street, on January 4, 1902.

 # George Scott McConkey

### # 46, plot U, lot 66

*A* native of Toronto, where he was born in 1841, George McConkey attended the old Upper Canada College on King Street West, west of Simcoe Street. He inherited the restaurant and confectionery business that had been started in Toronto by his father Thomas McConkey in 1840. On the death of Thomas in 1874, George opened a new restaurant at 145 Yonge Street, called McConkey's Restaurant, where he stayed for seven years before moving to the southeast corner of Yonge and Richmond Streets. Eight years later, he was forced to

move to larger premises at 27-29 King Street West. Still the business grew and in 1899 he purchased 31-33 King Street West effectively doubling the size of the popular restaurant. On September 27, 1904, George McConkey died in his residence on the second floor of the King Street restaurant.

# Henry A. Engelhardt

#47, plot E, sec 17 lot 1

*B*orn in Milhausen, Prussia in 1832, Engelhardt was educated in Berlin and graduated with a degree in civil engineering at the age of nineteen. He came to the United States in 1851 and took up residence in Baltimore, where he became a landscape gardener. It's believed Engelhardt came to Ontario about 1870 and over the next couple of years worked on several landscaping projects including laying out the grounds of the Ontario Institution for the Deaf and Dumb in Belleville as well as preparing plans for cemeteries in Belleville and Port Hope.

On June 17, 1874, eight months after the Trustees of the Toronto General Burying Grounds (now Toronto Trust Cemeteries) purchased 200-acres in York Township for a new cemetery, Engelhardt was hired by the trustees to prepare plans and supervise the laying out of fifty-three of the 200-acres that were to be officially opened in November, 1874 as the new Mount Pleasant Cemetery. Engelhardt was subsequently hired as the Cemetery Superintendent, a post he held until July of 1888 when, for reasons that are not totally clear, his employment with the cemetery was terminated by the Trustees.

There is no information about his circumstances during the next nine years until obituaries in the *Telegram* and *Globe* newspapers on November 10, 1897 revealed that the man responsible for the look of Mount Pleasant Cemetery and its first Superintendent had died in a rented room at 81 Richmond Street East on November 8, 1897. Henry Engelhardt was buried in a plot owned by the Trustees in "his" cemetery three days later.

**MOUNT PLEASANT CEMETERY**

# Samuel McBride

## # 48, plot D, sec 20 lot 8

*B*orn in the shadow of "Old City Hall" on July 13, 1866, Sam McBride was educated at Elizabeth Street and Wellesley Street Public Schools terminating his education at the age of eleven. He began delivering the *Leader* newspaper, then tried his hand at carriage painting followed by a short stint in the composing room of the *World* newspaper. He then got a job delivering lumber by horse and wagon. It was the appalling condition of many of the city's streets that convinced McBride that he should run for municipal office, so he could fight to get some of those thoroughfares fixed. His first attempt in 1905 was successful and he remained a ward Alderman until 1916 (except for the year 1909), then again in 1924 and 1925. He was a City Controller in 1917, 1918 and 1919, 1926 and 1932, 1933, 1934 and

1935. McBride was Mayor in 1928, 1929 and 1936. During the thirty-two year period from 1905 to 1936, McBride ran for office a total of thirty-one times and was successful on twenty-three occasions. It was in the spring of 1936 that Mayor McBride became ill and City Council approved an extended leave of absence. Over the next few months, the mayor made infrequent trips to his City Hall office and even talked on occasion about running in the following year's mayoralty race. However, on November 10, 1936, the seventy-year-old mayor suffered a severe stroke from which he never regained consciousness. Mayor Sam McBride passed away on November 14 at his home, 335 Inglewood Drive, the first chief magistrate in Toronto history to die while still in office.

# John Hallam

**# 49, Triangle 3**

*H*allam was born in Chorley, Lancashire, England on October 13, 1833. He was self-educated and emigrated to Toronto in 1856. He entered into the wool, hide and leather business and sat as Alderman for St. Lawrence Ward in 1870-1872, 1876-1883, 1888-1891 and for the renamed Ward Two in 1892-1899. During his second term on Council, and remembering his own educational deprivation, he secured the passage of the Public Library Act which led to the creation of the Toronto Public Library in 1884 with James Bain (PLOT R, LOT 32) as its first Chief Librarian.

Chorley Park in Rosedale, once the site of the Lieutenant Governor of Ontario's residence, had

**MOUNT PLEASANT CEMETERY**

been the property of John Hallam and was given its name in honour of the former owner's birthplace in England. Hallam had been the chairman of the city's Parks and Gardens Committee and over the years had imported many lovely flowers and shrubs into Canada. Hallam died as a result of complications of a severe asthma attack on June 21, 1900, at Linden Villa, his residence at 126 Isabella Street. John Hallam is buried with five other members of his family in an underground vault. Hallam Avenue in west Toronto is named for this civic-minded gentleman.

# Thomas Reid

#50, plot G, sec 14, lot 8

*B*orn in Ireland in 1845, Toronto fireman Thomas Reid died on January 14, 1887 at the age of forty-two. Due to the frost still being in the ground, the remains were interred in the cemetery vault until April 26, 1887 when the body was buried. Of particular interest is the memorial over Reid's grave. It is made of zinc, one of only a few of this type in Mount Pleasant Cemetery. On the memorial is a fireman's helmet and "piano action" fire engine, both of which identify Reid's occupation. Toronto's first paid fire brigade was organized in 1874, thirteen years before Reid died at the age of forty-two. The interment records indicate the cause of death was hemorrhaging of the lungs. Unfortunately there is no indication whether Reid died in the "line of duty".

# Adolphus Egerton Ryerson

#51, plot G, Triangle B

**B**orn on March 24, 1803 in the community of Charlotteville, Upper Canada (Ontario), Ryerson first attended the London District Grammar School in Victoria and, in preparation for becoming a lawyer, later moved on to the Gore District Grammar School in Hamilton. Ryerson suffered a serious illness in the winter of 1824-1825 and when he recovered decided to enter the Methodist ministry instead. He preached his first sermon on Easter Sunday, 1825, and, after many months as a missionary on the Yonge Street circuit, was fully ordained two years later. In 1829, Ryerson became the editor of the *Christian Guardian* newspaper which became one of the most influential papers in the young province. In 1840, he left the paper and

a year later became the first Principal of the new Victoria College, then located in Cobourg and which later moved to Toronto.

Dr. Ryerson was the "father" of the public education system in Ontario. In 1844, Ryerson became General Supervisor of Schools in Canada West (Ontario) and a year after that, 1845, the celebrated educationist made an extensive tour of schools in both Canada and the United States. As a result of this tour, Ryerson published an extensive report which advocated and described the organization of a province-wide public school. His report ultimately led to the Schools Act of 1871 which decreed that elementary schools would be tuition-free. The Act also established a set of criteria for mandatory school attendance.

Over the years, Ryerson continued to be deeply involved in all aspects of education culminating in Premier Mowat's (PLOT W, LOT 57) decision in late 1875 to create a provincial Ministry of Education.

Ryerson was also an accomplished and prolific author with many books and reports to his credit. Egerton Ryerson died at his residence, 171 Victoria Street, on February 19, 1882.

# John Medland

**#52, plot G, Triangle 8**

*B*orn in Devonshire, England on August 28, 1875, Medland came to Canada when he was six, settling in Port Hope, Ontario with his parents, where he attended the local public and high school. He joined his father in the retail grocery business in 1893, and in 1907 established Medland Brothers, Limited, wholesale grocers. When his company and twenty-five others joined together to form National Grocers' Company in 1925, Medland was appointed Vice-President. Three years later he was President and General Manager.

In late April, 1936, Medland and his wife journeyed to Boston, where they boarded the Bermuda-bound Canadian National steamship *Lady Hawkins*. On the morning of April 27, 1936, Medland awoke feeling under the weather. He went for a stroll on the deck and becoming disoriented, leaned against the railing and fell overboard. The ship's crew put about and searched for the victim and being unsuccessful, continued on with flag at half-mast. The Medland family monument describes the unfortunate incident with the words "DIED AT SEA".

 # William McMaster

*#53, plot G, lot 1*

*B*orn in County Tyrone, Ireland on December 24, 1811, young McMaster was educated at a local private school and at the age of twenty-two he emigrated to New York City. Soon after arriving in the United States, he decided to emigrate once again, this time to Toronto, or as it was still called, York. Here he obtained employment in the wholesale and retail shop of Robert Cathcart. McMaster was quickly invited to join his employer as a full partner. Just ten years later, McMaster struck out

on his own eventually becoming one of the most
respected wholesale dry-goods merchants in the
province. Business grew rapidly and soon after
McMaster retired from the dry-goods business, a
massive new warehouse bearing the name of his
successor, nephew A. R. McMaster, opened on the
north side of Front Street, just west of Yonge.
Though out of the mercantile business world,
McMaster remained active as the first President of
the Canadian Bank of Commerce, a position he
held for twenty years. He was also a director of
many other important financial institutions. Politically, McMaster ran for and won a seat on the
Legislative Council in 1862. When Canadian Confederation was passed in 1867, he was appointed to
the nation's first Senate where he represented the
Province of Ontario.

As a philanthropist, McMaster gave away
hundreds of thousands of dollars. He was also a
Trustee of the Toronto General Burial Grounds
(now Toronto Trust Cemeteries) from 1849 until
his death. He was responsible for the creation of
McMaster University (originally called the

Canadian Literary and Theological Institute) located in Woodstock, Ontario, Toronto's McMaster Hall on Bloor Street West, and Jarvis Street Baptist Church. William McMaster died at his 34 Bloor Street East residence on September 22, 1887 and was buried in Mount Pleasant Cemetery beside his first wife, Mary (d.1869). His second wife Susan Moulton McMaster (d.1916) was removed from the McMaster plot to Mt. Royal Cemetery in Montreal.

# William Mellis Christie

## #54, plot G, lot 9

*A* native of Huntly, Scotland, William Christie was born on January 5, 1829. He obtained a good education and then became a baker's apprentice while still quite young. Christie soon decided to seek out his future elsewhere and consequently came to Canada in 1848. Trying his luck first in the banking trade, he much preferred the bakery business and in 1849 joined the firm of Mathers and Brown, biscuit manufacturers.

The next year, Mr. Mathers retired and Christie became a partner with Alexander Brown. Then Mr. Brown retired, but rejoined the company eight years later. The enterprise was renamed Christie, Brown & Company, the name by which it is still known today. Brown retired for a second time in 1879, and William Christie carried on alone until he passed away at his residence, 29 Queen's Park (now Queen's Park Crescent East), on June 14, 1899.

In addition to his business interests, Christie was a staunch and avid supporter of the Toronto Industrial Exhibition (since 1912, the Canadian National Exhibition) and was intimately involved with its development since its formation in 1879.

On the death of his father, Robert Jaffray Christie took over as President, a position he held until his death on June 13, 1926, twenty-six years less one day after his father. His death occurred in the same house on Queen's Park Crescent. Also buried in the Christie family plot are William's wife Mary Jane (d.1909), Robert's wife Emma (d.1954) and their three children. Indicative of the mortality rates of the last century, three of William Christie's children who did not survive childhood are buried in a single grave.

# Franklin Doty

*#55, plot G, lot 5*

**A** native of Niagara Falls, New York, where he was born in 1849, Frank Doty moved to Hamilton, Ontario, then on to Toronto where he obtained employment in his father's shipbuilding and engine works factory. Here he helped build the two Toronto Island ferry boats Primrose and Mayflower, both of which were launched in 1890. The company also operated the Doty Ferry Company which boasted a total of eleven Island ferry boats including the little Luella, one of the most popular of all the Island boats. Luella was built by the Doty Company in 1882 and was named in honour of Frank Doty's first wife.

It was about 1893 that young Frank and his brother Fred decided to strike out on their own becoming involved in many enterprises in the bustling city of almost two-hundred thousand. One such venture was the operation of the quaint and popular Hotel Hanlan at the western tip of the Island.

In those days, as now, the city's drinking water was drawn from the lake south of the Island. On one of the hottest days of the summer of 1896, the large water supply pipe running under Toronto Bay from the Island filtration plant to the John Street pumping station (where Skydome now stands) broke. Frank and a few of his men were hired to fix the break. On the afternoon of August 6, 1896, while working on a hand-operated winch something went wrong and the handle kicked back, hitting Doty full in the face. The young man died a few hours later.

**MOUNT PLEASANT CEMETERY**

# Thomas Urquhart

#56, plot G, sec 4, lot 6

*B*orn in Wallacetown, Ontario in 1858, Thomas Urquhart attended the local public school until the age of thirteen, when he quit his studies and joined his father's tailoring business. Eventually, Urquhart returned to his studies and in 1886 graduated from Osgoode Hall as barrister and solicitor. In 1892, he became a partner in a Toronto law practice with his brother Daniel. In 1900, Urquhart was elected Alderman for Ward Four, a position he held until elected Mayor from 1903 until 1905. Urquhart then tried his luck provincially, only to be defeated on three separate occasions. Thomas Urquhart died from complications brought on by the dreaded influenza on February 16, 1931.

# Ann Preston

### #57, plot G, sec 9, lot 5

*L*ittle is known of Ann's early years, other than that she was born in Ireland in 1810 and became a servant in the home of Dr. and Mrs. J. Reid of Armagh. When the doctor and his family of ten emigrated to Upper Canada in the 1830s, Ann came with them. Dr. Reid purchased a house near the corner of Yonge and Elgin Streets in Thornhill, a small community just north of Toronto. When he and his wife died, Ann became the family housekeeper.

Even as a young girl, Ann Preston had shown a deep interest in the Methodist religion and even though she never learned to read, she could read the Holy Bible. In church, she would frequently cry out "praise the Lord" or "hallelujah" and when confronted on the street or in the local general store she would quote random passages from the Bible. Ann became the brunt of cruel jokes. One day, someone wrote in chalk on the Reid's front door "Holy Ann lives here. Go in and have a word". Though the words were used in derision, the epithet name "Holy Ann" stuck.

Throughout her long life, "Holy Ann" is reputed to have performed numerous "miracles", and when she died on June 21, 1906 at the age of ninety-six, ministers representing six different denominations paid tribute to Ann and her positive influence on others. One year after her death, a book documenting her life and work was published. Since then, the book has gone through twenty-eight editions and has been translated into five languages.

# William Fitch

#58, plot F, lot 8

*D*uring the Northwest Rebellion, the settlement of Batôche on the South Saskatchewan River was the site of the headquarters of Louis Riel and his Metis. On May 9, 1885 almost six thousand government troops under General Frederick Middleton attacked Batôche. The siege lasted three days and on the twelfth, Captain William Fitch of the Toronto-based 10th Royal Grenadiers was killed, as the official record states, "by a bullet through the heart". In total, seven government soldiers were killed during the Battle of Batoche. Riel surrendered to Middleton two days later. (SEE ALSO THE THOMAS MOOR-ISAAC HUGHES PLOT H, SEC 27, LOT A).

# James Aikenhead

## #59, plot F, lot 8

*B*orn in County Kilkenny, Ireland in 1816, James Aikenhead came to Toronto in 1847. Soon thereafter, he joined the firm of Joseph D. Ridout and Company, Ironmongers, which had been in operation since 1830. The company store was located at the northeast corner of Yonge and King Streets. In 1868, Aikenhead and Alexander Crombie became full partners in the business, which then changed its name to Ridout, Aikenhead and Crombie. Aikenhead and Crombie acquired control in 1876 and fifteen years later relocated the business to 6 Adelaide Street East. In 1893, James Aikenhead's son Thomas, who had begun his apprenticeship with the firm twenty years before, bought the business and again the name was changed, this time to Aikenhead Hardware Company. In 1901, the company was reorganized and renamed once more, this time to Aikenhead Hardware Limited. James Aikenhead, the founder died on April 11, 1903.

Two years after the death of James, the company moved to 17-21 Temperance Street where it was to remain for more than half-a-century. In 1944, James T.E. Aikenhead, the eldest son of Thomas who had died on April 3 of that year, became president, a position he held until his death on January 7, 1948. John Wilfred, Thomas's brother, then assumed the presidency holding the position until succeeded in 1972 by Thomas Aikenhead's nephew James Marley Aikenhead. John Wilfred died in 1984; James Marley in 1989. All five members of the Aikenhead family mentioned here are buried in the Aikenhead family plot.

*The Ridout, Aikenhead and Crombie hardware store, NE corner, Yonge and King Sts., c.1870.*

In 1972, the 142-year-old company was sold by the Aikenhead family. Still a very active enterprise, Aikenhead's is now owned by Molson Industries.

# John Fisher

## # 60, plot F, sec 6, lot 28

*P*erth, Scotland was the birthplace of John Fisher who emigrated to Toronto in 1856 at the age of twenty. Pursuing an interest in carpentry, Fisher moved to the Village of North Toronto where he obtained employment with Nicholas Maughan. He then went into partnership with James Ramsey and together they built numerous buildings in the village, which was elevated to town status in 1890. In addition to being a contractor, Fisher won the mayoralty race in North Toronto becoming that community's first Mayor, a position he held for thirteen years. The public school on Erskine Avenue is named for this respected citizen, who died at the Toronto General Hospital, then located on the north side of Gerrard Street just west of the Don River on May 27, 1911.

# Phillip Jamieson

## #61, plot F, lot 15

*A* native of Edinburgh, Scotland where he was born in 1850, Phillip Jamieson emigrated with his young wife to Toronto where he became a partner with his father-in-law Bartholomew Spain. Together they established the firm of Spain and Jamieson, wholesale and retail clothiers in a small store at 64 Queen Street West, near the corner of Terauley (now Bay) Street. When Mr. Spain retired, Jamieson became the sole proprietor and in 1876, moved the business into an old building at the northwest corner of Yonge and Queen Streets. That structure was badly damaged during the huge Simpson's fire that broke out on March 10, 1895 and destroyed a number of buildings including Robert Simpson's new store. Undaunted, Jamieson replaced his building with a new structure in which he ran his clothing store until his death at his 12 Beau Street residence on February 20, 1909.

It wasn't long after Jamieson's demise that the S. H. Knox Company's Five and Dime store opened

*Jamieson Building, NW corner of Yonge and Queen Sts., c.1897*

in Jamieson's "store with the rounded corner", as Torontonians referred to it. About 1912, the S. H. Knox store became an F. W. Woolworth store (Seymour Knox was a cousin of Frank Woolworth). Recently, the building was completely restored and modernized and a branch of the Royal Bank of Canada now occupies the main floor of the historic Jamieson Building.

 # Richard Ardagh
## #62, plot F, sec 7, lot 9

One of this city's most serious fires erupted early Sunday morning, January 6, 1895. Within twenty minutes the entire Globe newspaper building at the northwest corner of Yonge and Melinda Streets was in flames. In the course of fighting the fire one fireman was killed and Chief Richard Ardagh seriously injured. The latter's injuries were sustained when he was forced to jump from the third floor of a building next to the Globe.

Ardagh and two firemen were inspecting the neighbouring building when the south wall of the Globe structure gave way, striking the building in which the firemen were located. Forced to get out fast, all three jumped to safety. While the two firemen recovered from injuries sustained from their forty-five foot leap, the Chief was not so fortunate and died three weeks later on January 27, 1895. Because frost was in the ground, making the digging of his grave impossible, Ardagh was placed in a vault at Mount Pleasant Cemetery and buried on April 19, 1895. Ardagh Street in west Toronto was named for this valiant firefighter.

# George James Spring

*#63, plot F, sec 8, lot 8*

*T*his unusual monument marks the final resting place of Toronto-born and educated George Spring who founded the Dominion Wood and Coal Company in 1912. He died following a long illness on March 5, 1968.

# William Gage

## #64, plot F, lot A

*B*orn in Peel County and educated in Brampton, Ontario and at the Normal School in Toronto, Gage taught for three years before entering medical school. After only one year at the Toronto School of Medicine, he decided to enter the business world instead and joined the Adam Miller and Company publishing house. After Miller's death, Gage acquired the business and in 1876 later changed the firm's name to W. J. Gage and Company, an enterprise that is still in business under the Gage name. He also held directorships with many other business concerns.

Gage always had a special feeling for those afflicted with a disease called consumption (tuberculosis in modern day terminology) and in 1894 offered to build the first sanitarium in Canada. He founded the National Sanitarium Association and was responsible for the construction and equipping of the Cottage Sanitarium and Free Hospital in Muskoka, the Toronto Free Hospital for Consumptives (now West Park Hospital) and the Queen Mary Hospital for Consumptive Children on the banks of the Humber River in Weston, as well as the Free Dispensary at 223 College Street in Toronto (now known as the Gage Institute).

In 1917, Gage and his wife, the former Ina Burnside, gave $100,000 towards the establishment of the "Ina Grafton Homes" for the benefit of widows and children of Canadian soldiers. For his numerous philanthropic endeavors, Gage was knighted in 1918.

On January 14, 1921 Sir William Gage died at

his magnificent residence on the Davenport Hill in Wychwood Park. Interestingly, at one time, Gage had offered his house as the new Lieutenant Governor's residence. A site in Chorley Park was selected instead. Sir William Gage was originally buried in Plot F and removed to the new Gage mausoleum when it was completed in 1924.

Lady Gage, who continued her husband's philanthropic endeavors after his death, died in the residence on March 8, 1939. She was interred with her husband in the Gage mausoleum.

 # Albert Matthews

*#65, plot H, lot 9*

*B*orn in Lindsay, Ontario on May 17, 1873, Albert Matthews was educated in the local schools joining the Matthews-Blackwell Company, cattle dealers and meat packers in Ottawa when he was

just nineteen. He eventually took over the company's Toronto operations but soon decided to devote his future to the investment business, setting up his own company in 1909. Matthews was the President of Excelsior Life Insurance Company and the Chairman of McMaster University in Hamilton for twenty-five years. He also sat on a number of committees and was especially active in the Baptist Church. He was appointed the province's sixteenth Lieutenant Governor in 1937, retaining the Vice-Regal position until 1946. Albert Matthews died at his summer home on Lake Rosseau on August 13, 1949.

 # Thomas Moor and Isaac Thomas Hughes

**# 66, plot H, sec 27, lot A**

On May 16, 1887, a memorial was erected over the graves of Privates Thomas Moor and Isaac Thomas Hughes, both of whom died as a result of wounds received during the Battle of Batôche, the Northwest Rebellion's major conflict. The memorial was unveiled in the presence of 400 members of the late privates' regiment, Toronto's Tenth Royal Grenadiers.

Under Lieutenant H. J. Grasett, 271 Grenadiers had participated in the Battle of Batôche. One of their number, eighteen-year-old Moor, was killed in action on the first day of the battle, May 9, 1885 while Hughes, age twenty, succumbed on September 1, 1885 to wounds inflicted during the final encounter on May 12.

*First Ambulance Corps of the 10th Royal Grenadiers, 1885*

On the west side of the monument, in letters now almost completely obliterated by time and acid rain, are the words: "THE OFFICERS, NON-COMMISSIONED OFFICERS AND MEN OF THE ROYAL GRENADIERS, CONGREGATION OF ELM STREET METHODIST CHURCH, THE TEACHERS AND PUPILS OF RYERSON SCHOOL AND A FEW CITIZENS HAVE UNITED IN ERECTING THIS STONE TO THE MEMORY OF THOSE WHOSE NAMES ARE HEREON RECORDED AS HAVING LOST THEIR LIVES IN THE SERVICE OF THEIR COUNTRY." The fourteen-foot-high memorial was designed by Frank Darling, an ex-captain of the Royals. Also killed during the Battle of Batôche was Lieutenant William Fitch (PLOT F, LOT 8).

# Alice Margaret Kilgour

## # 67, plot H, sec 3, lot 3

*L*ittle is known of the early life of Alice Kilgour other than at the time of her death she was the widow of Joseph Kilgour. Joseph and his older brother Robert had established Kilgour Brothers, paper bag and cardboard box manufacturers in Toronto in 1874. Over the ensuing years, their company grew to become the largest business of its kind in the country.

Joseph Kilgour purchased a large tract of land on north Bayview Avenue which he called Sunnybrook Farm where he and Alice spent many pleasant years. In 1926, Kilgour died. Two years later his widow, the former Alice Margaret Grand, announced that she was giving to the citizens of Toronto 172 acres of land in memory of her husband. Sunnybrook Park was officially opened by Mayor Sam McBride (PLOT D, SEC 20, LOT 8) the following September. Alice Kilgour, the benefactress of Sunnybrook Park died on March 8, 1938.

In 1944, a portion of the park was transferred to the Federal Government and a new veteran's hospital was built. Sunnybrook Hospital opened on June 12, 1948. Some years later, the remaining City of Toronto park land was transferred to the Corporation of Metropolitan Toronto and is still in use as a Metro park.

*Sunnybrook Hospital is located on the Kilgour's Sunnybrook Farm.*

  # Patrick Close

## #68, plot H, lot 37

*B*orn in Ireland in 1838, Patrick Close came to Canada as a young man and entered the real estate business. For a period of time in the 1890s, he managed the Bedford Park Land Company that sold lots in North Toronto. During the period 1873-1878 and again in 1880, he represented the ward of St. Lawrence on City Council. In 1877, he was acting Chief Magistrate during the temporary absence of Mayor Angus Morrison. Close Avenue in the King-Dufferin area of the city is named for this gentleman who died at his residence, 253 Simcoe Street, on July 25, 1900 of blood poisoning brought on by an insect bite.

 **MOUNT PLEASANT CEMETERY**

# Thomas McGaw

**#69, plot I, lot 17**

*B*orn in Oshawa, Ontario in 1834, young Thomas
was educated locally before coming to Toronto,
where he worked at odd jobs before moving on to
Chicago. In May of 1862, while the Civil War was
raging south of the border and McGaw was still
living in Chicago, the British ship *Trent*, carrying
two Confederate officials to ambassadorial posts in
Great Britain, was attacked by a Union forces warship. The "Trent Affair" nearly precipitated war
between the Union forces and Great Britain. In
fact, the British Government ordered 14,000 dis-
patched from other posts to defend British North
America, while the Government under John A.
Macdonald and Etienne Cartier ordered out local
militia units totaling 40,000 men. Cooler heads
prevailed (Lincoln was having enough trouble with
the southern states) and the whole affair quickly
blew over.

Meanwhile, being a loyal Canadian, McGaw
had returned to Toronto where he signed up to
"fight for his country". When the "Trent Affair"
had been settled, he obtained employment as a
clerk at the Queen's Hotel on Toronto's Front
Street. In 1864, he and Thomas Winnett (MOUNT
PLEASANT MAUSOLEUM ROOM G) purchased
the hotel from its owner, Captain Thomas Dick.
Until his death on February 1, 1901, at his residence, 28 Avenue Road, Thomas McGaw was one
of the country's most popular and best-known
hotel owners. Twenty-eight years after McGaw's
death, the new Royal York Hotel opened on the
site of McGaw and Winnett's Queen's Hotel.

 # William Mortimer Clark

#70, plot I, lot 14

*B*orn in Aberdeen, Scotland on May 24, 1836, young Clark decided not to enter the family's insurance business, instead emigrating to Toronto when he was twenty-three. He studied law and was called to the bar in 1861, becoming a Queen's Counsel in 1887. On April 23, 1903, Clark was appointed Ontario's ninth Lieutenant Governor, a post he held until September 19, 1908. For his service to King and country, Clark was knighted in 1907. Clark was instrumental in ensuring plans to construct a new Knox College on Spadina Avenue came to fruition and he was also a founder of St. Andrew's College, then located in Rosedale.

Clark died on Friday, August 10, 1917 while on holiday at his summer home in Maine. His body was returned to Toronto by train and the funeral service was conducted at the Clark residence at 28 Avenue Road in a large house located where the Park Plaza Hotel now stands. Burial took place on Saturday, August 18.

Also buried in the Clark plot are Lady Helen Gordon Clark, Sir William's wife, their young son Gordon who died of diphtheria on January 20, 1902 and the couple's two spinster daughters Jean and Elizabeth. During the 1920s and 1930s, when virtually all traffic on the busy city streets was of the internal combustion variety, the two girls could be seen going about their business in an elegant horsedrawn carriage complete with coachman.

**MOUNT PLEASANT CEMETERY**

# Robert Emmett Kelly

## # 71, plot 2, lot 14

*V*ery little is known about the man for whom this mausoleum was built. What little we do know reveals that he was one of six sons born to Thomas Kelly, an Irish immigrant who settled in the United States in 1864, and subsequently made his way to Winnipeg, Manitoba. There Thomas Kelly became a building contractor and brick manufacturer. His construction company, Thomas Kelly and Sons, built many prominent structures in western Canada including the Legislative Buildings in Winnipeg. This latter project caused major problems for the Kelly family and when they were sued for bad workmanship, many of the Kellys took off for southern California.

All that is known about Thomas Kelly's son, Robert Emmett Kelly is that he married Bessie Olive Noden and died from the complications of pneumonia on April 29, 1915, while on his honeymoon in Atlantic City, New Jersey. Following his death, the new Mrs. Kelly had the mausoleum erected in his honour by the Thompson Monument Company at a cost of $8,000. Robert Emmett Kelly was interred in the mausoleum on December 28, 1916. There is a total of eight people in the Kelly mausoleum, including Robert Emmett's wife Bessie Kelly (d.1964), and Annie Parsons (d.1937), who was a friend of both the Kellys and Nodens. Having no family of her own, Annie was interred with her friends.

*T*oronto-born Matthew Sheard was the eldest of five sons born to Joseph Sheard, the Mayor of Toronto in 1871 and 1872. Joseph Sheard was an architect and contractor, though he refused to build the scaffolding from which Samuel Lount and Peter Matthews were hanged for their part in the Rebellion of 1837. As a young man, Matthew Sheard decided to follow in his father's footsteps and he too studied architecture. He practiced his profession in Toronto for thirty-five years, also doing work in Ottawa, New York City, Milwaukee and in Chicago, where he helped design buildings to replace those destroyed in the great conflagration that ravaged the "windy city" in 1871. One of Sheard's best-known Toronto works was the *Evening Telegram* newspaper office at the southeast corner of Bay and Melinda Streets. Matthew Sheard died on March 3, 1910 at his Yonge Street residence.

**MOUNT PLEASANT CEMETERY**

# George Tate Blackstock

### #73, plot 1, lot 70 & 71

*B*orn in Newcastle, Ontario in 1857 and educated at Upper Canada College, Blackstock was called to the bar in 1879. For a period of time, he acted as counsel for the Canadian Pacific Railway and in 1889 became a King's Counsel. He entered the field of criminal law and in 1890 defended Reginald Birchall in one of the most famous murder trials of the late nineteenth century. Birchall was charged with the cold-blooded murder of Frederick Benwell in the Blenheim swamp near Woodstock, Ontario. The trial, conducted in Woodstock, Ontario, caught the attention of people throughout North America and Great Britain, Benwell's birthplace. The motive for the murder was money - enough money for Birchell to place a wager on a horse in the Epsom Derby. The horse on which he wanted to bet won the race. But Birchall lost - his life. Even though Birchall was convicted and hanged, Blackstock's advocacy placed him in the highest esteem throughout the Canadian legal profession.

At the time of his death at his residence at 20 Homewood Avenue on December 27, 1921, he was with the firm Blackstock, Galt, Gooderham and McCann. He and eighteen members of the Blackstock/McKeggie/Horan families are interred in this unique underground vault, with the most recent burial taking place in the spring of 1985.

# Lionel Herbert Clarke

**#74, plot 2, lot 3**

$\mathcal{B}$orn in Guelph, Ontario on July 20, 1859, Clarke was educated at Trinity College School in Port Hope. Before he was appointed Ontario's twelfth Lieutenant Governor in November 1919, Clarke had been President of the Canada Malting Company and director of a number of other business enterprises.

With the formation of the Toronto Harbour Commission in 1911, he was appointed the organization's first Chairman. Ever since Clarke had moved to Toronto, he had always had a keen interest in the development of Toronto harbour. Long before the Harbour Commission was established, Clarke was promoting the adoption of public wharves rather than leaving them in the hands of a few private (and greedy) entrepreneurs. He also advocated the deepening of the harbour, so

ocean vessels could use the port. His plan was realized when the St. Lawrence Seaway finally opened in 1959. All this considered, it was not unusual that Clarke would continue as Harbour Commission Chairman even while holding the highest public office in the province. Lionel Herbert Clarke passed away at Government House, Chorley Park on August 29, 1921.

 # Ryland Herbert New
## #75, plot 2, lot 12

*B*orn in Toronto on July 16, 1888, Ryland New was educated at Lansdowne Public School, Harbord Collegiate, Upper Canada College and the University of Toronto. In 1908, he joined the Hamilton and Toronto Sewer Pipe Company, established many years before by New's father Jacob, as a salesman. In 1913, following the death of his father, New became president of the family company and fifteen years later amalgamated it with two other companies, Ontario Sewer Pipe in Mimico and Dominion Sewer Pipe in Swansea, to form the National Sewer Pipe Company. In 1987, the company sold off the manufacturing entities and became NSP Investments.

Ryland New had a passion for thoroughbred horses and two of his steeds, Troutlet and Aymond, won the King's Plate in 1927 and 1930 respectively. Ryland Herbert New died on November 21, 1979. Resting in the New mausoleum are ten members of the family including Jacob Herbert New who died in 1913 and was the first to be interred in the newly built structure.

# Simeon Heman Janes

**#76, plot 1, lot 30**

*A* native of Oxford County, Janes was born on February 5, 1843 and received his public and high school education in Ingersoll, Ontario. He graduated with a Masters Degree from Victoria College, then located in Cobourg, Ontario. He moved to Toronto in 1866, destined for the legal profession, or so he thought, but Janes soon developed a passion for real estate. In 1879, when the Toronto housing market was in a state of severe depression, he purchased large tracts of land which he judiciously subdivided, advertised and, as the market rebounded, sold at a large profit. One such area that Janes developed was the Annex in the Bloor/Avenue Road part of town. He also built a residence on the Avenue Road hill that he called Benvenuto. Simeon Heman Janes was sixty-nine when died of a stroke on July 4, 1913 in London, England, while completing an extended holiday. His body was returned to Toronto for burial. Also interred in the Janes plot are his wife Maria (d.1907) and daughters Eva (d.1924) and Louisa (d.1967).

**MOUNT PLEASANT CEMETERY**

# Robert Davies

#77, plot 2, lot 11

*B*orn in Toronto in 1849 and educated at Park School and Upper Canada College, then on King Street West, Robert Davies married the former Margaret Taylor. She was the daughter of John Taylor who owned and operated the Taylor Brick and Paper Works, located in the Don Valley near today's Pottery Road Bridge. Davies acquired both enterprises in 1901. He also owned the Dominion Brewery on Queen Street East.

Davies was an avid horseman and lover of the "sport of kings". One of his steeds, Kingston, won the Queen's Plate in 1871. For many years, Davies maintained a large racing establishment called Thorncliffe Farms in the Don Valley after which Thorncliffe Race Track and, later, Thorncliffe Park and shopping centre are named. At the time of his death on April 22, 1916, he lived in a residence called Chester Park on Broadview Avenue and was proprietor of the Don Valley Brick Works. Also buried in the family plot are Davies' wife and the couple's nine children.

*Just, formerly
Baillie Mausoleum.*

*T*his impressive mausoleum was originally built for Sir Frank Baillie who was born in Toronto on August 19, 1875. After a period of time as a clerk with the Central Canada Loan and Savings Company, Baillie was appointed private secretary to the company's founder George A. Cox, whose mausoleum is just along the way from this mausoleum. In later years Baillie organized his own brokerage company in Toronto. He was also President of the Burlington Steel Company, the Dominion Steel Foundry Company and, at the start of the First World War the Canadian Cartridge Company, the latter three being located in Hamilton, Ontario.

In 1916, Baillie was appointed Director of Aviation for Canada, Imperial Munitions Board and in the same month established Canadian Aeroplanes Limited which was created for the purpose of supplying the Royal Air Force with flying machines. He was knighted on January 9, 1918. While residing at 146 Crescent Road in Rosedale, he took sick on Christmas Day, 1920 and after a brief illness died at Wellesley Hospital on January 2, 1921. This mausoleum was built by his widow Lady Edith Baillie. In 1965, Sir Frank Baillie's remains were moved to St. Jude's Cemetery in Oakville, Ontario. The mausoleum then remained empty for many years.

In the early 1970s, the former Baillie mausoleum was purchased by the Just family and is now the final resting place of Gladys Irene Just (d.1970) and Gloria Irene Just (d.1977), daughters of Thomas Fullerton Just, a prominent mining equipment dealer who lived in Westmount, Quebec. The Just name is now found over the door where the Baillie name was originally located.

 # Frederick Nicholls

**#79, plot 1, lot 25**

*B*orn in England on November 23, 1856, Nicholls was educated in Germany before emigrating to Toronto, Canada in 1874. His first job was with a local newspaper before he accepted the position of secretary of the Canadian Manufacturers Association. Nicholls' prime interest was in the generation and sale of electricity. Assisted by Henry Pellatt (later Sir Henry) and William Mackenzie (later Sir

William), he established the country's first electric power company, the Electric Development Company, which generated electricity at Niagara Falls, transmitted it to Toronto where another of the trio's concerns, the Toronto Incandescent Light Company, distributed the power by underground cable. In 1892, Nicholls helped organize the Canadian General Electric Company He held the position of Vice-President and General Manager from 1892 until 1912, when he became President and continued to run the company until 1921 when he became Chairman of the Board. In addition to his affiliations with Canadian General Electric, Nicholls was President of the following companies: Canada Foundry, Canadian Allis-Chalmers, Marconi Wireless Telegraphy, Canadian Sunbeam Lamp. He was also Vice-President of the Toronto Railway Company, Toronto and Niagara Power Company, Toronto and York Radial Company, Dominion Coal Company, Dominion Iron and Steel Company, the Electrical Development Company and several others. His expert business acumen resulted in Nicholls being appointed to the Senate of Canada in 1917. Senator Frederick Nicholls died at his residence, 79 St. George Street, on October 25, 1921.

 # Edward Rogers Wood

## # 80, triangle 19

orn in Peterborough, Ontario on May 14, 1856, Wood was educated in the local public schools, before obtaining a full-time position as a telegraph messenger in the insurance office of George Cox (PLOT 2, LOT 8). Wood was still with Cox when

the latter organized the Central Canada Loan and Savings Company. When the business moved to the big city of Toronto in 1884, the twenty-eight-year-old Wood came with it. Before long, Cox's loan and savings company branched out to form the Dominion Securities Corporation. As the years went by, Wood advanced through the ranks, eventually becoming President of Central Canada Loan and Savings as well as of numerous other companies such as Brazilian Traction, Light and Power (now Brascan), National Trust and the Canada Life Assurance Company. He was a Director of the Canadian Bank of Commerce, Massey-Harris Company and a number of life insurance companies.

Wood was a generous man endowing the University of Toronto, both Victoria and Emmanuel College, Metropolitan and Sherbourne Street United Church and the Toronto General Hospital with large sums of money. He also worked diligently on the 1917 Victory Loan Committee bond drive and helped raise $600,000 for the Young Men's Christian Association.

In 1920, Wood and his wife moved to a newly constructed residence he called Glendon Hall on Bayview Avenue in York Mills. Following Edward Rogers Wood's death on June 16, 1941 at the age of seventy-five, his wife Agnes continued to reside at Glendon. On her death in early 1950, Glendon Hall was bequeathed to the University of Toronto and in 1961 became the first building on the campus of the newly established York University's Glendon College. Both Edward Rogers Wood and his wife Agnes are buried in the Wood plot at Mount Pleasant Cemetery.

# George Albertus Cox

## #81, plot 2, lot 8

*Cox Mausoleum, flanked by those of the Eaton and Baillie (Just) families.*

*B*orn in Colborne, Ontario on May 7, 1840 young George was educated in the local elementary school. Following graduation, he obtained a job as a telegrapher for the Montreal Telegraph Company. Two years later, he was promoted and put in charge of the company's Peterborough office. Cox took an active part in the political life of Peterborough holding the office of Mayor for seven years. In 1878, at the age of thirty-eight, he helped negotiate funds for the reconstruction of the Midland Railway, becoming President of the company in 1878. Six years later, the refurbished railway was sold to the Grand Trunk Railway with the shareholders (including Cox) earning substantial profits.

Later, he became associated with the Canada Life Assurance Company and founded the Canada Loan and Savings Company in 1884. In 1888, Cox moved to Toronto where he continued to dominate the business world. Amongst other positions, he

**MOUNT PLEASANT CEMETERY**

was President of the Canadian Bank of Commerce, the Canada Life, British America and Western Assurance Companies, the Toronto Savings and Loan Company as well as a Director of numerous other important enterprises such as the Toronto Railway Company and Toronto General Trusts. He was so important in financial circles that in 1909 he was described by the press as being one of the most influential businessmen in the country. He was also philanthropic, giving thousands to organizations such as the Toronto General Hospital, the Victorian Order of Nurses and the Methodist Church. Cox was called to the Senate of Canada in 1896.

Early in the morning of January 16, 1914, Senator Cox passed away at his 439 Sherbourne Street residence. A total of sixteen people have been interred in the Cox mausoleum, including the Senator's two wives, Margaret (d.1905) and Amy (d.1915), the senator's six children, plus financier A. E. Ames, the senator's son-in-law and husband of daughter Mary.

 # Alfred Ernest Ames

**# 82, plot 2, lot 8**

*A*. E. Ames was born in Lambeth, Ontario in 1867. Investment banking was comparatively new at that time and Ames was a pioneer in the field. He began his business career in the Merchants Bank in Owen Sound and over the next few years held various positions in a number of banks, returning to Toronto in 1889, where he started his own financial business which he called A. E. Ames Company.

Soon he became involved in the brokerage business entering the area of municipal and government bonds early in this century. Again he was a pioneer. It was due in large measure to Ames' diligence that Canada's first Victory Loan in 1917 was an unqualified success.

Ames' large estate on the Kingston Road, complete with a nine-hole golf course, was called "Glen Stewart" and it was here that he passed away on September 20, 1934. Two streets in the area recall Alfred Ernest Ames, Glen Stewart Avenue and Glen Ames Road.

 # Muriel Billes

### #83, plot 3, lot 32

*M*uriel Moore was the daughter of printer-turned-land developer Delford Moore. On December 13, 1928 Muriel Moore became Muriel Billes when she married Alfred Jackson Billes.

"A.J.", as he was better known, and his older brother, John William Billes, opened their Hamilton Tire and Garage Company on Hamilton Street just south of Gerrard on September 15, 1922. The following year, they moved to a store at Yonge and Gould Streets in downtown Toronto followed quickly by another move uptown to the northeast corner of Yonge and Isabella Streets. In 1927, the boys moved across Isabella and opened a store at 637 Yonge while at the same time incorporating under a new name, Canadian Tire Corporation Limited. And the rest, as they say, is history. Muriel Billes died on August 13, 1979.

# Charles Seward Blackwell

#84, plot 2, lot 6

*B*orn in Lindsay, Ontario in 1857, Blackwell operated a grocery store in that central Ontario community from 1883 until 1892. Moving to Toronto,
he established the Park-Blackwell provision business which merged in 1912 with the George Matthews Company and Laing Packing and Provision
Company to form Matthews-Blackwell Ltd. Their
processing plant was located at the foot of
Bathurst Street, east of Fort York and for years,
before the plant was expropriated, blocked the
extension of Bathurst Street to the waterfront.
Blackwell was Vice-President of the company until
it was purchased in 1919 by Allied Packers of
Chicago. Two years later, he was appointed to the
Board of Directors of the Toronto General Hospital
becoming Chairman of the organization in 1931.
He was also Chairman of the Board of the Dominion Bank. He was well respected for his philanthropic gestures. Blackwell died while on holidays
in London, England on June 23, 1932, and was
brought back to Toronto for burial.

 # John Thomas Moore

## #85, plot 2, lot 5

*A* native of the Township of Markham, where he was born on July 3, 1844, John Moore was educated in Toronto and Berlin (now Kitchener), Ontario. In 1883 and 1884, he sat on Toronto City Council as an Alderman for St. Paul's Ward. It was Alderman Moore's motion, put forward on May 19, 1884, that resulted in Toronto's new City Hall being erected at the top of Bay Street.

Moore was also the Managing Director of a ill-fated Toronto real estate project called the Belt Land Corporation that spawned the Belt Line Railway. A portion of this steam railway operated through the easterly portion of Mt. Pleasant Cemetery. Both the corporation and railway lasted less than two years before a drastic decline in land prices forced the project into bankruptcy

In 1905, Moore moved west and was elected as the first M.P.P. for Red Deer, Alberta, the province having been newly created out of a portion of the Northwest Territories. Moore remained an M.P.P. from 1905 until 1909. Two years later, Moore spearheaded the construction of the Alberta Central Railway and became the line's first President.

Several years later, he returned to Toronto and settled in the district he had established called Moore Park. His Avoca Vale was a place of beauty and well known for the extensive rose gardens Moore had planted.

John T. Moore died in his Ernscliffe Apartment building, which still stands at the southeast corner of Sherbourne and Wellesley Streets, on June 15, 1917.

145

**MOUNT PLEASANT CEMETERY**

# George Locke
## #86, plot 2, lot 5

*M*oore's son-in-law and the Toronto Public
Library's Chief Librarian George Locke is also
interred in the Moore family plot. Locke was born
in Beamsville, Ontario on March 29, 1870. Moving
to Toronto as a child, Locke was educated at Ryerson Public School in Toronto and at the Brampton
and Collingwood Collegiate Institutes. He then
returned to Toronto and attended Victoria university and the University of Toronto obtaining his
M.A. in 1896 and LL.D. in 1927. Locke went on to
teach at the prestigious American colleges, Harvard, Radcliffe, University of Chicago and Canada's
McGill University in Montreal. In 1908, he was
appointed the Toronto Public Library's chief librarian. It was under Locke's guidance that Toronto's
existing public library system, with its dimly-lit
and uninviting main building, four cramped
branches and staff of twenty-six was transformed
into one of the most modern, efficient and popular
library organizations in the world. During Locke's
term as Chief Librarian, the new Central Reference
Library at College and St. George Streets and the
nearby Boys' and Girls' House were opened.

When George Locke died at the Wellesley
Hospital at the age of sixty-seven on January 28,
1937, the library system he had nurtured could
boast sixteen branches and a staff of 232. Locke
married Alice Moore, John Thomas Moore's daughter. She died on May 28, 1948 and is also interred
in the Moore plot.

#87, plot 2, lot 4

*B*orn in 1836 on a small farm a couple of miles north of the town of Ballymena in Ireland, Timothy Eaton was the youngest of nine children born to John and Margaret Eaton. The hard-working father never did see Timothy, however. John Eaton died from an illness contracted while helping a farmer friend. Margaret named the fatherless son after one of the John's favourite books of the New Testament. As a young man, Timothy was apprenticed to a prosperous merchant in the nearby small town of Portglenone where he put in sixteen-hour days and six-day weeks. When Timothy had enough of the famine and misery prevalent throughout the land and working long hours for someone else, he decided to make a change. With a hundred pounds in his pocket, he struck out for promises of the "new world" across the ocean.

**MOUNT PLEASANT
CEMETERY**

*Sir John Eaton*

From 1854 until 1868, he lived in various Ontario towns, working and operating small dry goods stores. Eventually, Timothy joined his two brothers Robert and James who had been running their own grocery and dry goods store in the town of St. Mary's. In 1860, the trio decided to split up, with Timothy and James retaining the dry goods and millinery departments while Robert remained in the grocery business. Two years later Timothy met and married the former Margaret Beattie of Woodstock.

In 1868, Timothy made one of the most important decisions of his young life. He would take his family and move to the big city of Toronto (population somewhat less than 50,000) where he would open his own dry goods store. Forced into a short stint in the wholesale dry goods business, which Timothy truly disliked, the thirty-three-year-old finally got his chance to go it alone when he purchased for the sum of $6,500 the business of James Jennings at the southwest corner of Yonge and Queen Streets, far from the hustle and bustle of the retail heart of the city down on King Street. In his first advertisement, Eaton startled Torontonians with the statement that rather than bartering for the best price or buying on credit, goods in

Eaton's new store would be sold at a fixed price and for cash only. This is commonplace enough today, but in 1869 those concepts were highly unusual.

As the years went by, benchmarks in the fascinating Eaton's story came and went: the move north of Queen Street in 1883, the first Eaton catalogue in 1884, the company's first telephone in 1885, the first elevator in 1886, early store closings on Saturday in the same year followed by the creation of a mail order department, buying offices in foreign countries, company owned and operated manufacturing factories and so on. By January 1, 1907, the T. Eaton Company, under the control and guidance of the founder, had become the most important and influential department store in the entire Dominion.

On January 31 of the same year, Timothy Eaton died from the complications of pneumonia at the age of seventy. The funeral procession, moving through crowd-lined streets from the family residence at 182 Lowther Avenue to the newly constructed family mausoleum at Mount Pleasant Cemetery, was comprised of more than 200 carri-

*John David Eaton*

ages, a large number of the "new-fangled motors" preceded by several thousand mourners on foot.

Also interred in the family mausoleum are three of Timothy and Margaret's children who died while babies (Timothy Jr., ten months, Kate, eleven months and George who drowned at twenty-two months,), twenty-six-year-old Lillie and thirty-seven-year-old Edward. Another son, Sir John Craig Eaton (d.1922), who was knighted in 1915 for his numerous philanthropic endeavors during both war and peacetime, is also in the mausoleum. He was company President from 1909 until his death in 1922. Also interred within is John David, John Craig's second eldest son who was President from 1942 until he retired in 1969 and turned control of Eaton's over to his two sons John Craig and Frederik Stefan, both of whom are still very much alive. Robert Young Eaton, Timothy's nephew, who "looked after the store" from 1922 until 1942, is across the way in PLOT 3, LOT 3. Others in the mausoleum include Timothy's wife Margaret (d.1933) and Sir John's wife Lady Flora McCrea (d.1970). The most recent interment was Timothy Craig (d.1986), Sir John Craig's eldest son and John David's younger brother who could have been

*Robert Young Eaton*

*The Eaton Mausoleum soon after Timothy was interred. The structure is now almost hidden by mature trees.*

President, but opted for a life of leisure rather than one of business headaches. Interestingly, Timothy Craig had requested that he be buried in Ballymena, Ireland, where his grandfather, the namesake and founder of Eaton's had been born.

In total, there are sixteen people interred in the Eaton family mausoleum.

 # Foster Hewitt

### #88, plot 3, lot 7

*F*oster Hewitt was born on November 21, 1902. He was the son of William "Billy" Hewitt, sports editor for the Toronto Star where, after graduation from the University of Toronto, Foster obtained a job writing a weekly column on the newest wonder of the age - radio. One afternoon, Foster was despatched to Mutual Arena where he was to repair broadcast equipment installed by the newspaper's radio station CFCA He was also told to be ready to broadcast that evening's O.H.A.

senior playoff hockey game between teams from
Kitchener and Toronto, if no one else could be
found. No one was found, so on the evening of
March 22, 1923 Foster Hewitt broadcasted his
first hockey game. Coining the never-to-be-
forgotten words, "He shoots, he scores!", Foster
Hewitt remained Canada's "voice of hockey" for a
lengthy fifty-six years. In addition to hockey
games, Hewitt also broadcast wrestling matches,
football games and marathon swims held off the
C.N.E.'s waterfront. Without doubt, the event that
gave Hewitt his biggest thrill was the final game
in the Canada-U.S.S.R hockey final in 1972, when

Toronto Maple Leaf Paul Henderson scored the winning goal for Team Canada.

Hewitt was also a shrewd businessman. In 1951, Foster purchased a small Toronto radio station CKFH (the "FH" stood for Foster Hewitt) and sold it twenty-nine years later for $4 million. He was also Vice-President of CFTO-TV, part-owner of the Vancouver Canucks hockey team and director of several mines in northern Ontario. Foster Hewitt died on April 22, 1985, at the age of eighty-two.

# James Franceschini

### #89, plot 3, lot 4

*W*hen fifteen-year-old James Franceschini arrived in Canada from his hometown of Pescara, Italy in 1906, the young man spoke virtually no English and was totally penniless. Befriended by a Toronto city policeman who found Franceschini a place to sleep that first night, the youngster found himself a job the very next day. Franceschini soon earned enough to buy a horse and wagon and eventually began his own small excavation company. Time passed and the young man could soon afford to add a steam shovel to his equipment list. He suffered a major financial setback in 1916, but was able to recover and within a decade was the country's largest road contractor. One of his many enterprises was called Dufferin Construction.

In 1939, Canada went to war and Franceschini did his part by establishing the Dufferin Shipbuilding Company at the foot of Spadina Avenue. Here he contracted to build minesweepers

for the Government, but suddenly, and as it turned out, without proof, James Franceschini was arrested, fingerprinted and consigned to an internment camp as an enemy alien. Investigations subsequently proved Franceschini's innocence, but a full year went by before he was granted a pardon. Due to government ineptitude (as a result of what was later proven to be blatant racism), Franceschini's release was held up for another five months. Finally, a physician's report on the deteriorating health of the Canadian citizen gained him his release. Once free, Franceschini purchased an estate in the Laurentians, where he died on September 16, 1960.

 # John Stanley McLean
## #90, plot 3, lot 14

*B*orn on a farm near Port Hope, Ontario on May 1, 1876, young McLean was educated locally before attending the University of Toronto, where he graduated in 1896 with his Bachelor of Arts degree. After teaching in Lindsay, Ontario for a couple of years, he joined the Harris Abattoir in Toronto as an accountant-bookkeeper. Within four years, he rose to the position of Secretary-Treasurer and was elected as one of the company directors. In 1927, McLean merged four companies - the Harris Abattoir Company, Gunns Limited, Canadian Packing Company, and William Davies Company - into the new Canada Packers Limited. with fifty-year-old McLean as President, a position he held for twenty-seven years. On August 11, 1954, he turned the company over to his son and exactly three weeks later, September 1, 1954, the seventy-eight-year-old McLean passed away suddenly at his palatial residence, 2225 Bayview Avenue, following a heart attack.

The house, designed by the late Eric Arthur, is now used by the Sunnybrook Health Centre as a conference and reception centre.

# Roscoe R. Graham
## #91, plot 3, lot 23

*B*orn in the small hamlet of Lobo, Ontario in 1890, Graham was the son of Dr. Peter Graham, a traditional country doctor. After completing his studies in the local school system, the young Graham moved to Toronto where he attended the University of Toronto and graduated with a degree in medicine at the age of twenty.

During the First World War, Graham served with the Royal Canadian Medical Corps returning at the cessation of hostilities to join the staff of Toronto General Hospital. Graham became a leading authority in the field of abdominal surgery and in 1939 was called on by American specialists to perform an extremely delicate surgical procedure on Edsel Ford, head of the Ford Motor Company empire. The operation was a complete success. Graham became one of Toronto General Hospital's senior attending surgeons and was Assistant Professor of Surgery at the University of Toronto. On January 17, 1948, while skiing with friends on the slopes near Collingwood, Ontario, the fifty-eight-year-old doctor was stricken with a massive heart attack. He died almost instantly.

# Willard Garfield Weston

#92, plot 5, lot 2

*A young Garfield stands next to his father George in this c.1904 family portrait.*

*F*ollowing the death of his father George (PLOT 19, LOT 27), twenty-six-year-old son Garfield Weston took over the business and within a year, sales had tripled. The younger Weston was born in Toronto in 1898 and educated at Harbord Collegiate. In 1917, he joined the army and spent two years overseas. Upon his return, he joined the family company and worked in every department, so that when he assumed the presidency of the company on his father's death he knew the biscuit and cake business thoroughly. In 1933, Weston moved to England where there were more than one hundred biscuit makers. Within ten years, Weston's was the biggest in the country. Weston branched out and bought the E. B. Eddy Company, the William Neilson Company, the late Theodore Pringle Loblaw's supermarket empire and several other interests.

In addition to his business dealings, Weston was a philanthropist donating millions to various charities including a million dollars to the Banting and Best Department of Medical Research at the University of Toronto. During the Second World War, he wrote a cheque for $400,000 to cover the cost of sixteen Spitfire aircraft shot down in a recent air raid. Weston also served as a British Member of Parliament.

For a time, Weston owned the former residence of steel magnate Frank Wood on Bayview Avenue. Weston sold the property in 1967 to the owners of a private learning institution and now Crescent School occupies the house. Garfield Weston died on October 22, 1978 at the age of eighty, while visiting his hometown. His son Galen now manages the Weston empire.

 # Charles Rathgeb

### #93, plot 5, lot 1

*I*n 1949, the Canadian Comstock Company, of which American-born Charles Rathgeb was founder and President, was requested by the Hydro Electric Power Commission of Ontario (now Ontario Hydro) to undertake a massive province-

wide frequency standardization program. The job of converting the electrical equipment of seven million Hydro customers from twenty-five to sixty cycles was initially estimated as a fifteen year project. Canadian Comstock, which was involved at the time with the electrification of Canada's first subway, the T.T.C.'s Yonge line, completed the colossal $352 million job in just ten years. Charles Rathgeb was subsequently involved in the construction of the Trans-Mountain Oil Pipe Line, the Trans-Canada Microwave System and the St. Lawrence Seaway. He died at the age of seventy-three, while vacationing in Florida on April 5, 1969 and was returned to Toronto for burial.

# Mount Pleasant Mausoleum, Crematorium and Chapel

*L*ocated directly east of Plot 4 on the south side of the cemetery is the Mount Pleasant Mausoleum, Crematorium and Chapel. Work on this impressive structure began in 1917 and the first phase of the mausoleum opened on February 6, 1920. It was designed by the architectural firm of Darling and Pearson, a company that was also responsible for the Toronto General Hospital on College Street, the Bank of Commerce Building on King Street West (for many years the tallest building in Canada) and

*Architect's sketch of the proposed Mausoleum.*

Convocation Hall on the grounds of the University of Toronto.

John A. Pearson, one of the partners in the firm of Darling and Pearson, is buried in Mount Pleasant Cemetery (PLOT 10, LOT 20).

The exterior of the mausoleum is faced with Stanstead granite quarried in Quebec, while the interior is Italian marble, bronze and glass. Originally the chapel was used during the winter months when it was impossible to dig graves due to frost in the ground. Following the service, the remains were stored in the mausoleum until interment could be carried out in the spring. Modern equipment now permits interments year-round.

In 1973, a modern crematorium was added and ten years later expansion of the original mausoleum structure allowed for increased interment capacity as well as on-site office space. The original chapel has been renamed the Carfrae Chapel and a newer Ewart Chapel was built as part of the 1983 mausoleum expansion project. They have been named in honour of two of the Trust's original members, Thomas Carfrae, Jr. and John Ewart.

**MOUNT PLEASANT
CEMETERY**

# William G. Barker

**#94, Mount Pleasant Mausoleum
room B, crypt B**

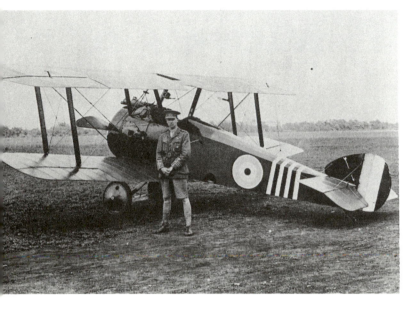

One of Canada's greatest war heroes, Colonel Barker destroyed fifty enemy aircraft during the First World War becoming Canada's second ranking air ace. In addition to being awarded the Distinguished Service Order and Military Cross and Bars, Barker also received the coveted Victoria Cross.

Born in Dauphin, Manitoba in 1894, Barker was killed on March 12, 1930, when a Fairchild biplane he was testing crashed at the Ottawa Airport. Burial took place on the fifteenth from Barker's father-in-law's residence at 355 St.Clair Avenue West. During the service, six Toronto Flying Club aircraft flown by First War pilots skimmed over the grave site and released thousands of rose petals as their tribute to one of the nation's most distinguished war heroes. In 1931, a small airfield on the west side of Dufferin Street north of Lawrence Avenue was named Barker Field in memory of Colonel William Barker.

 # Charles Luther Burton

## #95, Mount Pleasant Mausoleum
## room E, crypt C

*B*orn in Malvern, Scarborough Township in 1876, Burton and his family moved to Toronto in 1899. The young man enrolled in Jarvis Collegiate, then located south of Carlton Street, but quit school at the age of fifteen and obtained employment as an office boy in a law firm. Before long, he left and obtained a similar position with Fancy Goods of Canada Co. Ltd. which was owned by H. H. Fudger. Burton worked his way up the proverbial ladder, years later becoming its Managing Director. In 1912, Burton became Assistant General Manager at the Robert Simpson Company, then under the directorship of his old friend and mentor H. H. Fudger. By 1929, Burton was President of Simpson's, becoming Chairman of the Board in 1948 when his son Edgar assumed the presidency. Burton was an advocate of a two language society in Canada and often declared that every Canadian student should be proficient in both English and French even before learning arithmetic. Charles L. Burton died on March 19, 1961 at his residence, 136 Glen Road.

# Mary Fortune

**#96, Mount Pleasant Mausoleum
room C, crypt 103**

*O*n the evening of April 14, 1912, the stately *R.M.S. Titanic* ploughed its way across the North Atlantic, striving, some said, to set a new trans-Atlantic speed record. At precisely 11:40 p.m. that evening, the huge vessel struck a massive iceberg and in less than three hours the ill-starred *Titanic* slipped beneath the waters of the cold Atlantic taking 1,513 to their icy graves.

When *Titanic* set sail from her Southampton, England port on April 10, 1912, six passengers were from Winnipeg, Manitoba. Mark Fortune had taken his wife Mary and their four children Ethel, Alice, Maud and Charles with him on his business trip to Great Britain. The return trip on the maiden voyage of the White Star Line's newest ship was to be the highlight of the Fortune family's trip. When the extent of the loss of life after the great ship foundered was finally established, two of the dead were Mark Fortune and his young son Charles. Mary and the girls were fortunate to be counted among the pitifully meager list of survivors that in total amounted to just 711.

Following her rescue, Mrs. Fortune was reported as confirming that one of the passengers in her lifeboat was a man dressed in woman's clothing. Some years later, Mary Fortune moved to Toronto and resided at 7 Rose Park Crescent, where she died on March 8, 1929.

# Albert Edward Kemp

#97, Mount Pleasant Mausoleum
private room H - I

*B*orn on a farm near Clarenceville, Quebec on August 11, 1858, young Edward Kemp was educated in the local school system before striking out on his own in the big city of Montreal. In 1885, he decided to move to Toronto where he soon became a partner in a small company called Sheet Metal Products Limited. Two years later, Kemp became sole owner. Thanks to the young man's business acumen, the company thrived and was sold in 1927 to General Steel Wares for more than $3 million. Kemp was elected to the Federal Parliament representing East Toronto in 1900, and again in 1904 and 1911. In that latter year, he became a

**MOUNT PLEASANT
CEMETERY**

member of the prestigious Privy Council and was re-elected by acclamation in 1916 and again the general election of 1917.

During the first World War, Kemp was appointed Chairman of the War Purchasing Commission and as such was responsible for saving the country millions of dollars through judicious buying and shrewd bargaining. He even returned wages that he earned as a public servant during the war years. In 1916, Kemp became Minister of Militia and Defence and a year later, Minister of Overseas Military Forces, retaining this latter position until all the troops had been demobilized. It was also in 1917, that Kemp was knighted by King George V. After the war, he was one of Canada's representatives at the Peace Congress at Paris. In 1921, he was called to the Senate of Canada by Governor General Lord Byng. Back in Toronto, Kemp was one of the founders of the Art Gallery, a regent of Victoria College, a governor of the University of Toronto and Honourary Lieutenant-Colonel of the Toronto Regiment (3rd Battalion, C.E.F.).

It was early in the morning of August 12, 1929, while holidaying at his summer home called Mississiquoi on Pigeon Lake and the day after celebrating his seventy-first birthday with Lady Kemp and his family, that Sir Albert Edward Kemp died. His body was returned to Toronto and a private funeral service was held on August 14, 1929, in the family's Toronto residence Castle Frank prior to his interment in the Mount Pleasant Mausoleum. Castle Frank was located on Castle Frank Crescent near the site of the original Castle Frank of Governor John Graves Simcoe.

# Thomas Alexander Russell

*Tommy Russell (behind steering wheel at extreme left) and a quartette of Russell automobiles in front of Toronto's City Hall, 1905.*

**B**orn in Exeter, Ontario on April 17, 1877, Tommy Russell received his early education in the local schools before attending the University of Toronto, graduating in 1899. After a short stint with the Canadian Manufacturers Association, he joined Canada Cycle and Motor Company in 1903. The next year, C.C.M. established a new company to

**MOUNT PLEASANT CEMETERY**

produce Canada's first successful automobile. The Russell Motor Car Company, of which Tommy Russell was President, continued to turn out Russell cars from their Weston Road plant until 1915, when the company merged with Willys-Overland Limited. During the First World War, the Russell part of the company manufactured shells, fuses, aircraft parts, armoured cars and trucks at three separate plants, one of which was located in Buffalo, New York.

In 1930, Russell was appointed President of the Massey-Harris Company, a position he held for ten years. In addition to holding several company presidencies, he was also a Director of the Canadian Bank of Commerce, Mutual Life Assurance, Canada Cement, Canadian Vickers and the Canadian National Exhibition, becoming President of this latter organization from 1918 to 1920. Russell was also a Governor of his old alma mater and a Trustee of the Toronto General Hospital. He was an expert agriculturist and frequently livestock from his six hundred and fifty-acre Brae Lodge farm in Downsview would win first prize at shows held all over North America. On December 29, 1940, Thomas Alexander Russell died at his residence, 1 Dewbourne Avenue, at the age of sixty-three.

# Augusta Stowe-Gullen

### #99, Mount Pleasant Mausoleum
### room 60, crypt E

*B*orn in Mount Pleasant, Canada West (Ontario) on July 27, 1857. As a girl, she came to Toronto and was eventually accepted into the Toronto School of Medicine. She went on to Victoria University in Cobourg and back to Toronto's Trinity College. In 1883, Augusta Stowe became the first Canadian woman to have studied medicine and graduated with a medical degree from a Canadian university. Years before, her mother Dr. Emily Stowe had studied medicine in Canada, but was forced to obtain her medical degree from an American institution. A few years later, Dr. Stowe introduced the suffrage movement into Ontario that ultimately resulted in women obtaining the right to vote.

Augusta Stowe married Dr. John Gullen, one of the founders of Western Hospital on Bathurst Street, after her graduation in 1883. For the next seven years, 1883 until 1890, Dr. Stowe-Gullen was a demonstrator in anatomy at the Ontario Medical College for Women after which she was appointed lecturer, then professor of diseases of children at the College. She was also connected with the Western Hospital.

In addition to her medical affiliations, Dr. Stowe-Gullen also championed women's issues serving as President of the Ontario Provincial Council of the National Council of Women for a period of four years, after which she was elected Vice-President of the National Council. She also sat on the Senate of the University of Toronto for twelve years. Dr. Augusta Stowe-Gullen died at her residence, 461 Spadina Road, on September 25, 1943 at the age of eighty-five.

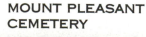

# George Howard Ferguson

# 100, plot 4, lot 1

*B*orn in Kemptville, Ontario on June 18, 1870, Ferguson attended the local schools for a time, but because of his prankish behavior was eventually sent to Toronto for further schooling. Following completion of his studies at the University of Toronto and Osgoode Hall, Ferguson was called to the bar in 1894.

Returning to his hometown in eastern Ontario, he entered municipal politics first as an Alderman and subsequently Reeve. In 1905, Ferguson ran provincially, winning a seat for the Conservative Government. Over the following years, he held various positions within the government including the important post of Minister of Education. Elected party leader in 1920, Ferguson and his party won a majority of seats in the election of 1923, with Ferguson then assuming the premiership. He held that office for seven years relinquishing the reigns of office to his successor George S. Henry in 1930. For the next five years, having declined an offer to become Federal Conservative leader, Ferguson was the Canadian High Commissioner to London. He retired from public life in 1935, though he accepted the post of Chancellor of the University of Western Ontario in 1945. During Ferguson's seven year tenure as the Premier of Ontario, Ferguson saw the creation of the provincial liquor control system and the Liquor Control Act, expansion of the hydro-electric and provincial highway networks and helped resolve a long-standing dispute over the teaching of French in Ontario schools. On February 21, 1946, at the age of seventy-five, the Honourable Howard G. Ferguson died of heart failure at his 559 Avenue Road residence.

# Alfred Russell Clarke

## # 101, plot 1, lots 3, 10

*B*orn in Peterborough, Ontario on October 7, 1859, Alfred Clarke was employed in the family leather business. When his father died, the nineteen-year-old moved the company to Toronto in 1882 where he established A. R. Clarke & Company, first on Francis Street (off King Street near the St. Lawrence Market) and quickly moving to larger quarters on Eastern Avenue. The company

was incorporated seventeen years later in 1899 with Mr. Clarke as President.

On May 1, 1915, Clarke journeyed to New York City where he boarded the magnificent Cunard transatlantic liner *Lusitania* bound for Liverpool, England and a week long business meeting. Six days out and within sight of the Irish coastline, the huge vessel was torpedoed by the German submarine U-20. In less than eighteen minutes Lusitania was no more. A total of 1,198 passengers and crew were killed. One of the survivors was Alfred Clarke who, though soaked to the skin from his ordeal in the water awaiting rescue, telegraphed his family that he was safe and on his way to London.

A slight head cold quickly developed into pneumonia and on June 20, 1915 the unconscionable sinking of the ill-fated Lusitania had claimed another victim. Clarke's body was returned to Toronto and buried on July 7, 1915. The A. R. Clarke Company continues in operation on Eastern Avenue though it passed out of Clarke family control in 1977.

 # Gerhard Heintzman
## # 102, plot 1, lot 13

*B*orn in Osnabruk, Germany in 1848, Gerhardt Heintzman (no relation to Theodore Heintzman PLOT T, LOT 10) emigrated to the United States at the age of nineteen. He worked for a number of years with various American piano companies before moving to Toronto in 1867, where he estab-

lished his own manufacturing plant on Sherbourne Street. At its peak, the Gerhardt Heintzman Piano Company employed more than two hundred skilled piano craftsmen. The factory still stands at the northeast corner of Sherbourne and Adelaide Streets, with the main floor occupied by a fine restaurant. After a short illness, Gerhard Heintzman passed away at his residence, 75 Binscarth Road on October 6, 1926.

# William Barclay McMurrich

## # 103, plot 1, lot 45

*B*orn in Toronto on November 1, 1842, the young McMurrich was educated at the old Knox Academy, Upper Canada College on King Street West and at the University of Toronto, where he

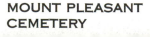

graduated in 1863, receiving his Master of Arts the next year. McMurrich went on to study law and was called to the bar of Ontario in 1866.

Two years later, he was elected School Trustee for St. Andrew's Ward and vigorously supported the idea that Toronto's public school system should be available to students free of charge. In 1877, he resigned as Trustee and was appointed the Board of Education's solicitor, a position he held for more than thirty years. McMurrich went back into municipal politics again in 1879 when he was elected Alderman for the same ward which he represented as School Trustee. He was re-elected ward Alderman in 1880 and one year later decided to run for Mayor. Again he was successful and retained the Chief Magistrate's position again in 1882. McMurrich resigned his position in 1883 to contest that year's federal election for the riding of West Toronto, which he lost. McMurrich had numerous business connections and at various times was a Director of The Globe newspaper and President of the Nipissing and James Bay Railway. He was also active in Presbyterian church work and in the city's musical life, being Vice-President of the Conservatory of Music for many years. William Barclay McMurrich was also a Trustee of the Toronto General Burial Grounds (now Toronto Trust Cemeteries) from 1883 until his death which occurred at his Lake Joseph, Muskoka summer home on September 6, 1908. McMurrich's younger brother James Playfair McMurrich, an internationally famous scientist and Professor Emeritus of Anatomy at the University of Toronto, is also interred in the McMurrich plot. He died at his residence, 20 Foxbar Road, on February 9, 1939 at the age of eighty.

# Elias Rogers
## # 104, plot 1, lot 46

*B*orn a few miles north of Toronto in Whitchurch Township on June 23, 1850, Elias Rogers was educated in Newmarket and at Cayuga College in New York State. He first entered the lumber business, then switched to coal and purchased the first mines to open in Jefferson County, Pennsylvania. In 1876, he and his brother Samuel opened a retail coal business under the name Elias Rogers Company. In 1887, he served a one-year term as Alderman for St. Lawrence Ward and then was defeated the following year when he ran for Mayor of Toronto. In addition to his own business, Rogers was President of the National Life Assurance Company, Vice-President of the Imperial Bank of Canada and a Director of many companies including National Trust and the Dominion Iron and Steel Company. Elias Rogers died on April 11, 1920 at his large residence called Glen House on the east side of Yonge Street, just south of Mt. Pleasant Cemetery.

# John Fensom
## # 105, plot 1, lot 61

*E*migrating to the United States while still a young man, John Fensom eventually made his way

to Toronto and began working in a small machinery shop. In the early 1870s, Fensom started his own company where he specialized in the manufacture of elevators. The head office of his new company was located in the former home of Chief Justice Sir William Campbell's residence on Duke (now Adelaide) Street with the factory in buildings located behind the old house. (Campbell House now stands at the northwest corner of Queen Street and University Avenue.) In 1905, the Fensom Elevator Company amalgamated with the Otis Elevator Company to become the Otis-Fensom Elevator Company, now Otis Canada, Incorporated. Soon after the amalgamation, Fensom retired and died at his residence, 540 Sherbourne Street, on August 23, 1908.

 # J. Milton Cork

## # 106, plot O, lot 17

*C*oming to Toronto as a boy from his hometown of Picton, Ontario where he was born in 1870, Milton Cork obtained his elementary education in the Toronto public school system. At the age of sixteen he began working in his father's grocery store at 335 King Street East. It was here that a young fellow named Theodore Loblaw from Alliston, Ontario found a job a few years later. Loblaw and Cork became good friends and soon each opened his own grocery store. A few more years went by and in 1919 the boys decided to pool their resources and try something new in Canada, the self-serve grocery store. If it hadn't been for Cork's desire to remain behind the scene, shoppers today

might be buying meats and groceries at Cork's. Instead, the name Loblaw's became synonymous with the term supermarket. Following the death of T. P. Loblaw in 1933, Cork became President, then Chairman of the Board. He died at the age of eighty-seven at his Old Forest Hill Road home on April 21, 1957, with the funeral service the following Tuesday.

 # Robert John Fleming

#107, plot O, lot 14

*A* true "cabbagetown" boy, Bob Fleming was born on St. David Street on November 23, 1854, and attended the old Park School, but quit before

**MOUNT PLEASANT CEMETERY**

graduating to accept a position of office boy at $3 per week. He then entered into partnership with T. W. Elliott in the coal and wood business. In 1886, he took a fling at municipal politics and was elected Alderman for St. David's, his home ward. After being re-elected in 1889, he served a second term, after which he dropped out to do some speculating in the real estate business.

Fleming was drawn back to politics and in 1892 was elected Mayor. He was defeated in 1894, but ran again in 1896 and won. He was re-elected in 1897, but resigned to take up the position of Assessment Commissioner for the city. In 1904, he requested a raise from $4,000 to $6,000 per year, was refused and quit. He was instantly hired by the Toronto Railway Company, who operated the city's streetcar fleet, at an annual wage of $10,000 and for the next seventeen years, when the privately-owned T.R.C. was taken over by the Toronto Transportation Commission, acted as the company's General Manager. In 1923, Fleming again ran for the position of Mayor, but was defeated by less than a thousand votes.

For many years, Fleming lived at the northeast corner of Bathurst Street and St. Clair Avenue, which he bought for $5,000 as a cattle pasture when his neighbours next door to his house on lower Parliament Street complained about his keeping his herd in the backyard. In June of 1924, he moved again, this time to the former estate of W. F. McLean called Donlands, on the Don Mills Road. It was here that he died on October 26, 1925.

 # Lionel Cutten

## # 108, plot O, lot 18

One of the most unique monuments in the cemetery is this work by German-born sculptor Emanuel Hahn who is also responsible for such Toronto landmarks as the Ned Hanlan statue in Exhibition Place and Sir Adam Beck's likeness in the median of University Avenue, just south of Queen Street.

The Cutten family memorial was crafted by the Thomson Monument Company in their studio at 862 Dupont Street from a thirty-two ton block of Laurentian pink granite quarried near Guenette, Quebec. The finished weight of the memorial, which took ten months to sculpt, approximates twenty-one tons and was moved from the Thomson studio to the Cutten plot on July 23, 1936. The two women reposing on the bench represent Annie Rowena Cutten, wife of Lionel Cutten and her sister, Helen Gertrude Moncur. The two ladies died less than a year apart, October 16, 1932 and January 6, 1933 respectively. The memorial was commissioned by Annie's husband, Lionel Cutten.

Lionel Cutten, who is also buried in this plot, was born in Guelph, Ontario in 1871. While still a young man, he came to Toronto where he and Anthony Foster established Cutten and Foster, importers of automobile parts, radios and drapery manufacturers. Cutten's brother was Arthur Cutten, a well-known grain merchant known throughout the States as "the wheat king". Lionel Cutten died of a heart attack at his residence, 118 Forest Hill Road, on August 21, 1938.

**MOUNT PLEASANT CEMETERY**

# J.McPherson Scott

# 109, plot N, sec 7, lot 4

*B*orn in Ayr, Ontario on February 24, 1859, Scott received his primary and secondary education in Galt and then attended the University of Toronto, where he graduated in philosophy in 1877. Twelve years later, Scott graduated from Knox College and was ordained Minister of St. John's Presbyterian Church in east central Toronto. On December 23, 1913, while the Rev. Scott was walking along Broadview Avenue, he was shot at by a deranged religious fanatic. Of the six bullets that were shot at him, three missed, two were deflected by a steel eye glass case Scott habitually carried in his left breast pocket, while a third bullet struck Scott in the hip injuring him.

The extraordinary work carried out by Rev. Scott during his many years as Minister of St. John's prompted an organization that had been formed in 1908 as the Christian Synagogue to change its name to the Scott Institute. Now located at 502 Spadina Avenue, it is known as the Scott Mission. J. McPherson Scott died at his residence, 537 Broadview Avenue, on February 25, 1920, just one day after his sixty-first birthday.

# Warring Kennedy
## # 110, plot J, lot 16

*B*orn in County Down, Ireland on November 12, 1827, young Kennedy went to school in Londonderry before apprenticing in the dry goods business in a small shop in the Town of Kilrea. Then it was onto Belfast and ten years later the thirty-year-old emigrated to Toronto, Upper Canada where he obtained employment in the Golden Lion dry goods emporium located on the south side of King Street on the site of today's King Edward Hotel. After a time, he joined the firm of Senator John Macdonald, "the merchant prince" and worked there for short time before he joined with two other young gentlemen in the same company to form the new dry goods firm of Sampson, Kennedy and Gemmel. Later, as simply Sampson and Kennedy, the firm came to be regarded as one of the finest in the country.

**MOUNT PLEASANT CEMETERY**

In 1871, Kennedy tried his hand at municipal politics and was elected Alderman for St. John's Ward. He ran for the position of Mayor in 1877, but was defeated, returning for another try in 1894, when he defeated R. J. Fleming (PLOT 0, LOT 14). He defeated Fleming again in 1895 by the slimmest majority in the city's political history, forty-five votes. Following this second term as Toronto's chief magistrate, Kennedy returned to private life and accepted a number of company directorships, was the first president of the Commercial Travelers' Association and sat on the boards of the House of Industry, Hospital for Incurables and the Irish Protestant Association. He was also a Trustee of the Toronto General Burying Ground Trust (now Toronto Trust Cemeteries), a position he held from 1876 until 1904. It was early in the morning of June 25, 1904, when Warring Kennedy passed away at the home of his sister, 91 Spencer Avenue in Parkdale.

 # Joseph Shepard II
## # 111, plot J, sec 7, lot 2

*W*ho says Sheppard and Wilson don't come together? They do when they're a married couple. Joseph Shepard II and Elizabeth Willson were longtime residents of York Township. Joseph owned a large 200-acre parcel of land on the south side of today's Sheppard Avenue between Leslie Street and Don Mills Road from 1849 until 1872. He was a son of the Joseph Shepard I who acquired 400-acres of land at the northwest corner of today's Yonge Street and Sheppard Avenue in the early 1800s. The concession road fronting the elder Shepard's property took his surname, though with a slightly altered spelling. About 1860, his son Joseph Shepard II built the general store that still (1990) stands at the northwest corner of Yonge and Sheppard Avenue.

As for Elizabeth Willson, she was a descendent of John Willson I who had emigrated to Upper Canada during the American Revolutionary War. He obtained land on Yonge Street in York Township. All of Willson Senior's sons, John II (who helped build St. John's Anglican Church, York Mills), Stilwell, William, Isaac and Jonathon, became prominent landowners in the township as did many of their descendants. One of the Willson daughters, Elizabeth, married into the Shepard family thereby bringing Shepard and Willson together. Over the intervening years, the spelling of the Shepard and Willson surnames was changed slightly when the names were affixed to a pair of the township's muddy east-west thoroughfares. Joseph Shepard II died on April 24, 1899, at the age of eighty-four.

# Harry Edward Foster

### # 112, plot N, sec 11, lot 22

*B*orn in Toronto on March 1, 1905, and educated at Ridley College in St. Catharines, Harry "Red" Foster founded his highly successful Foster Advertising Agency in 1944. He actually began his career as a sports announcer covering wrestling matches, football, speedboat and lacrosse events coast-to-coast. He introduced Canadians to the first outdoor radio theatre in the country at the Cana-

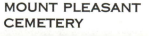

dian National Exhibition and was rated as the second best speedboat driver in the world. In addition to being involved in numerous business interests and having received countless accolades from his peers, Foster was probably best known for his interest in and support of the mentally retarded through the Harry E. Foster Charitable Foundation and the Special Olympics for the mentally handicapped. As a youngster, Foster had grown up with a mentally handicapped brother, Jack. The boys' mother spent much of her waking hours attending to Jack's needs. His mother's dedication so impressed young Harry, that as he grew older, he too dedicated himself to assist with the welfare of Canada's mentally handicapped. Harry "Red" Foster died on January 18, 1985.

 # Frank Westwood

## # 113, plot J, sec 12, lot 16

*L*ate in the evening of October 6, 1894, there was a knock at the door of the Westwood residence at 28 Jameson Avenue in the recently annexed Parkdale neighbourhood of Toronto. Eighteen-year-old Frank Westwood, son of Benjamin Westwood of the fishing tackle and sporting goods firm of Allcock, Laight and Westwood, answered the door. Without speaking a word, a figure dressed in male attire pointed a gun at young Frank and pulled the trigger. A shot rang out, Frank fell back into the house and the gunman fled into the cold night air. Both of Frank's parents quickly responded to their son's cries for help and within minutes a doctor who lived nearby was tending to the young man's injuries. On the morning of October 10, just four days after the shooting he lapsed into a coma and died. The police were without a suspect until one of the Westwood's neighbours pieced together some scraps of paper he found in a pile in his garden. A few pieces were missing, but a cryptic message made up of the following five words was decipherable "If you don't —— I will". A reporter for a local newspaper got wind of the neighbour's find and used the note in a follow-up story on the unsolved murder. The article prompted a reader to suggest to police that it might be worth questioning a young woman who occasionally dressed in men's clothing, carried a revolver and had been an acquaintance of the murdered young man.

Clara Ford was brought in for questioning and after finding all sorts of incriminating evidence in her small flat, the young woman confessed to the crime claiming that Westwood had frequently made improper advances to her. The police were convinced they had an iron-clad case. But when the crafty Clara was brought before the judge and jury, she claimed she'd been coerced by the police into pleading guilty. The very fact that the young man had made those advances would mean Clara would be acquitted and this is what the authorities had assured her. The judge was outraged and quickly set Clara Ford free. She was never seen again. Young Frank Westwood's cold-blooded murder has never been avenged.

# John Charles Smith

## # 114, plot J, sec 15, lot 24

*The Smith home (centre) at 175 University Ave., c.1910*

*L*ittle is known about John Smith other than at his death on February 11, 1898 at the age of thirty-one, he was married to the former Charlotte Hennessey, had three children, Gladys Marie, Lottie (short for Charlotte) and Jack Jr. The Smith family lived in a small house at 175 University Avenue, near the corner of Elm Street. One day, the young father of three suffered a severe head injury when he struck his head on an overhanging pulley either at the Rising Sun Hotel on Yonge Street where he was a barkeeper, or on the lake steamer *Cibola* where he was employed in the warmer months as a concessionaire. (History is

184

vague on exactly where Smith met his end). He was momentarily knocked into unconsciousness and when he recovered he was sent home. Later that evening, Smith went into convulsions and died.

The grieving widow, recognizing the need for a new source of income to keep her family together, decided that the eldest daughter, four-year-old Gladys, who had shown some acting talent, might be able obtain employment as a child actress. Following a visit to New York City and an encouraging conversation with prominent American theatrical producer David Belasco, Charlotte Smith decided to give her daughter a new name to help insure Gladys' success on the stage. She chose "Mary" from Marie and "Pickford" from grandfather Hennessey's middle name. As "America's Sweetheart" wrote in her biography, had her father John Charles Smith not died when she was still a youngster, there would never have been a Mary Pickford, the world's first "movie star".

# John Severn

**# 115, triangle 9**

*B*orn in Derbyshire, England in 1807, young John Severn arrived in Upper Canada in 1830 and settled in the Town of York (Toronto) where he continued to practice his trade as a blacksmith. A year went by and Severn decided to move out of the little community of less than 4,000 and venture up Yonge Street to the community known as Yorkville. Here he built for himself a small blacksmith forge. In 1832, Severn got into the brewing business and purchased the defunct brewery of a local resident John Baxter. Severn enlarged the structure on several occasions and operated a very successful business until his death in 1880.

In addition to being a brewmaster, Severn was active politically, being elected one of the newly created Village of Yorkville's first four Councilors in 1853. The initial "S" and a keg of beer can still be seen on the original Yorkville coat-of-arms now affixed to the front of the firehall on Yorkville Avenue. Severn was re-elected Councilor in 1859 and held the position through to 1863 and again in 1867. From 1868 until 1877, he served as Reeve of Yorkville.

John Severn died on February 8, 1880. Also interred in the Severn plot are John's three wives, Jane (d.1842), Aureta (d.1868) and Jane Wilson (d.1874). It is said that the six pillars that form part of the monument represent Severn, his three wives and his two children all of whom predeceased him. Severn Street is named for this Yorkville pioneer.

 # Hart Almerin Massey

## # 116, triangle 7

*W*ithout question, the Massey mausoleum is the most imposing structure in Mount Pleasant Cemetery. Designed by famed Toronto-born architect Edward James Lennox (of "old" City Hall, King Edward Hotel and Casa Loma fame), the two-tiered structure was completed in 1891 for

*Hart Almerin Massey*

the interments of Hart Almerin Massey's two sons, Frederick Victor and Charles Albert Massey.

Hart Massey was born on the family farm in Ontario's Northumberland County on April 29, 1823, the eldest son of Daniel Massey. The youngster received his early education in Watertown, New York, subsequently entering Victoria College (then in Cobourg, Ontario) and graduated in 1844. In 1849, his father left the farm and established a small foundry and machine shop in Newcastle, Canada West (now Ontario) where two years later, young Hart took over as Manager. In 1879, the company, renamed the Massey Manufacturing Company (later the Massey-Harris Company and now Varity Corporation), moved to a new six-acre site near the Exhibition Grounds in Toronto. The story of the growth of this internationally famous farm implement manufacturing concern is legendary.

On February 12, 1884, Hart's thirty-five-year-old son Charles Albert died after contracting

*Massey Hall, erected 1894*

typhoid fever. In his memory, the grieving father built Massey Music Hall on Shuter Street which opened on June 14, 1894. Six years after the eldest son's death, Hart Massey's youngest son Frederick Victor died on April 17, 1890, from complications brought on by tuberculosis. In his memory, the father established the Fred Victor Mission which opened on October 26, 1894. Hart Massey, who in addition to building these two city landmarks also gave large amounts of money to many churches and charitable organizations, died on February 20, 1896.

All three Masseys are interred in the family mausoleum along with Hart's younger brother George Wentworth Massey (d.1854) who was only one-year-old when he died and who was originally buried in Newcastle before being moved to Mount Pleasant Cemetery in 1901.

Also in the Massey family mausoleum are

Anna Vincent Massey (d.1903), Hart's wife Eliza Ann Massey (d.1908), John Mill Treble (d.1909), daughter Lillian Massey Treble (d.1915), Margaret Phelps Massey (d.1921), Hart's second son Chester Daniel Massey (d.1926) and Walter Seldon (d.1946), a close family friend.

Chester Daniel Massey was a great benefactor in his own right and was responsible for building the University of Toronto's Hart House which was named in honour of his father. Lillian Massey financed the construction of the Lillian Massey School of Household Science Building at the southeast corner of Bloor Street and Avenue Road. On the triangle of land surrounding the mausoleum are interred the remains of eleven other members of the Massey family, including Hart's third son Walter Edward Massey (d. 1901), who was originally interred in the family mausoleum and then buried beside his wife at the time of her death, his wife Susan (d.1938) and their son Denton Massey (d.1984), founder of the extremely popular York Bible Class for Young Men.

189

**MOUNT PLEASANT CEMETERY**

# John Smith

## # 117, triangle 5

*B*orn in Germany, Smith came to Toronto in 1841 at the age of twenty-two. Little is known of his early life. But his obituary does reveal that through hard work in his newly adopted city, in both the wholesale and retail grocery trade and in the shoe manufacturing business, Smith was able to accumulate a large amount of money. In addition to serving on City Council in 1877, 1878 and 1879, representing St. James' Ward, retiring on account of ill health, Smith was also a director of several financial institutions.

It was after visiting a property in Weston, Ontario on behalf of one of these companies that Smith met his untimely end while homeward bound on the evening of September 29, 1881. A coroner's jury determined that after leaving a northbound horse-drawn CHURCH streetcar one stop north of his customary stop, Smith crossed the dimly lit thoroughfare, proceeded south on the west side, towards his residence at number 35 Isabella Street. It was surmised that in the darkness Smith tripped over a pile of scoria blocks being used to repair the street, fell, then staggered onto the southbound streetcar tracks where he fell again and collapsed into unconsciousness. The streetcar from which he had just alighted, having come to the end of the route, began its return run downtown. Unable to see any obstruction on the track ahead, the operator urged his horses on. Without any apparent warning, the horsecar ran over the body of Smith killing him instantly.

 # Robert Jaffray

### # 118, plot L, lot 6

*B*orn near Bannockburn, Scotland on January 23, 1882, Jaffray was educated at the famous Stirling Academy and worked for a time in Edinburgh before emigrating to Canada, where he entered the retail and wholesale grocery business in Toronto. Jaffray developed an interest in railways and was appointed director of many such enterprises. He was also affiliated with such diverse companies as Globe Publishing (in 1936 it merged with the *Mail and Empire* to become the *Globe and Mail*), Canadian General Electric, Canada Life and the Toronto General Trust Corporation. Jaffray was called to the Senate of Canada by Governor General Earl Grey on March 8, 1906. Several weeks prior to his death, he was elected President of the Imperial Bank of Canada. Robert Jaffray died at his residence Surrey Lodge, 78 Grenville Street, on December 16, 1914.

# James Michie

## # 119, triangle 4

*T*he youngest of seven children, James Michie was born in Corryhoul, Scotland on February 27, 1828. At the age of seventeen, he and his brother came to Canada, where they obtained employment with A. Ogilvie and Company, wholesale and retail grocers, where James Michie's uncle George Michie was a partner. In 1852, James Michie and A. T. Fulton were admitted into the business as full partners. Within a few years, the wholesale and retail sides of the business were separated and, with the subsequent death of both Alexander Ogilvie and George Michie, James Michie took charge of the retail trade in a store called Fulton, Michie and Company on King Street West. Eventually, both sides of the firm came under the control of Messrs. Fulton and Michie. For the next half-century the shop at 7 King Street West, which was renamed Michie and Company after the death of Fulton, was one of the most popular and successful grocery stores in the city. It closed in the early 1950s.

James Michie, the grocer, was also a Director of the Bank of Commerce, the Western Assurance Company and the Dominion Telegraph Company and was a Trustee of the Toronto General Burial Grounds (now Toronto Trust Cemeteries) from 1874 until his death. He had major financial investments in other business ventures and donated great sums of money to numerous charities. He died at his residence, 36 Wellington Place (now that part of Wellington Street west of Spadina Avenue), on January 13, 1883.

 # Viola Thompson

#### # 120, plot E, lot 9196

On Thursday, July 19, 1934, the body of Viola Thompson was found under a lilac bush on the north side of Blythwood Road near the corner of Bayview Avenue by a trio of youngsters seeking shelter under the bush from an afternoon shower. Those many years ago, the Bayview-Blythwood area was described in the coroner's report as being very much a country setting and Blythwood Avenue simply a rough, badly lit country road. An autopsy conducted on the body revealed that the young woman had died as a result of numerous severe blows to the head.

Shortly after the body was discovered, the husband of the murder victim, Alwynne Thompson, was arrested by Toronto police following a tip that Thompson had obtained a marriage license after claiming to be single while still married to Viola. The license had been issued the day before his wife's body was found. It was determined by forensic experts that Viola Thompson, whose true identity was unknown for days, died on July 19, 1934. She was buried eight days later in the shadow of the cemetery's north wall. Though many felt that Alwynne Thompson, who served time on the perjury charge, had killed his wife, the murderer of Viola Thompson has never been apprehended.

**MOUNT PLEASANT CEMETERY**

# William Lyon Mackenzie King

# 121, plot L, sec 46, lot 21

*B*orn in Kitchener (then called Berlin), Ontario on December 17, 1874, King was the son of lawyer and Osgoode Hall lecturer John King (d.1916) and his wife, the former Isabel Grace Mackenzie (d.1915), daughter of William Lyon Mackenzie, the "fiery rebel" and leader of the Rebellion of 1837 in Upper Canada. He attended public and high school in his hometown before enrolling at the University of Toronto where he graduated with a B.A. in 1895, L.L.B. in 1896 and M.A. in 1897. He also won fellowships at the University of Chicago and Harvard. When Mackenzie King wasn't attending university, he worked as a newspaper reporter and frequently wrote about social problems and conditions. He was offered the position of Deputy Minister in Prime Minister Laurier's new Labour Department which the young man accepted. In 1908, Mackenzie King was elected to Parliament for the first time as the Liberal member for Water-loo North and was subsequently appointed Minister of Labour. In 1911, both Mackenzie King and his party were defeated, and he soon left for the United States where he became Director of Industrial Research for the Rockefeller Foundation.

In 1917, Mackenzie King returned to Canada and ran unsuccessfully as the Liberal candidate in the riding of York North. Following the death of Sir Wilfrid Laurier in 1919, Mackenzie King became the new leader of the national Liberal Party. He won a seat in a by-election in Prince County, Prince Edward Island and in the general election of 1921 decided to run again in York North where he had been defeated four years earlier. This time he won and was now able to sit in parliament as the country's tenth Prime Minister.

In 1925, another election was called, but this time the outcome was indecisive. The Liberals tried to carry on, but the balance was too precarious and Parliament was dissolved. The Conservatives under Arthur Meighen formed a government only to be defeated in the general election of 1926 (having been in power a mere eighty-eight days). Mackenzie King once again took over, this time remaining in the prime minister's office until defeated by R. B. Bennett in 1930. Five years later, Mackenzie King and his Liberals were again returned to power, as they were following elections in 1940 and 1945. In total, William Lyon Mackenzie King held the office of Prime Minister of Canada for more than twenty-one years, a record that still stands. He relinquished the party leadership and prime ministership in 1948, though he retained his seat in Parliament until the general election held on June 27, 1949. A little more than one year later, on July 22, 1950, Mackenzie King passed away and was laid to rest with his mother (with whom he is said to have communicated after her death) and father in Mount Pleasant Cemetery five days later. A total of nine people are interred in the King plot.

# George W. Beardmore
# 122, plot L, sec 4, lot B

*B*orn in Hamilton, Ontario in 1851, Beardmore
was educated at Upper Canada College, then
located on King Street West in downtown Toronto.
He was the founder of Beardmore and Company,
Tanners and Leather Merchants on Front Street
East. The company's warehouse at 35-39 Front
Street East still stands, beautifully restored to its
1872-73 glory. With his deep interest in horseman-
ship, he helped found the Toronto Hunt Club.
Beardmore resided at "Chudleigh", a noble 1872
residence at 136 Beverley Street that is now
occupied by the Italian Consulate. Beardmore died
at Wellesley Hospital on October 10, 1934.

# Resting Place of the Pioneers

*L*ocated at the east end of PLOT K is a boulder on
which there is a special commemorative plaque to
the dozens of "pioneers" who were moved to this
area of Mount Pleasant Cemetery in the early
years of Mount Pleasant's development. These
pioneers were originally interred in the Toronto
General Burying Ground's first cemetery at the
northwest corner of Yonge and Bloor Streets. As
the community in and around Potter's Field (as the

old cemetery was called) grew in size, the cemetery's location became a problem. As a result, in the mid-1850s the government ordered that the site be cleared to permit redevelopment. Many of the remains were transferred to the Necropolis on the west bank of the Don River, while almost 300 unclaimed remains were reinterred in the new Mount Pleasant Cemetery which was still being developed and a year away from its official opening. With the Potter's Field site cleared, the Trust's first cemetery closed in 1875. It wasn't until almost a century later that a plaque commemorating the memory of approximately 300 of our community's early pioneers was unveiled.

# Noel Clifford Marshall
## # 123, plot L, sec 13, lot 34

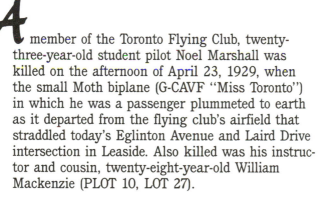

*A* member of the Toronto Flying Club, twenty-three-year-old student pilot Noel Marshall was killed on the afternoon of April 23, 1929, when the small Moth biplane (G-CAVF "Miss Toronto") in which he was a passenger plummeted to earth as it departed from the flying club's airfield that straddled today's Eglinton Avenue and Laird Drive intersection in Leaside. Also killed was his instructor and cousin, twenty-eight-year-old William Mackenzie (PLOT 10, LOT 27).

The Toronto Flying Club had been organized in 1928 and continued to use the Leaside airfield until 1931, when the redevelopment of the area as an industrial subdivision made its operation unsafe.

# Alexander Muir

## # 124, plot X, lot 12

*B*orn in Lesmahagow, Scotland in 1830, Muir was just a baby when the family emigrated to Canada and settled in the wilds of what is now Scarborough. Years later, he attended Queen's University, and at the age of twenty obtained a teaching assignment in an old schoolhouse out near the tiny community of Agincourt at the north end of the Scarborough Township. Ten years later, Muir was teaching in Leslieville on the eastern outskirts of Toronto.

One day in the fall of 1867, he noticed a newspaper advertisement placed by the Caledonian Society of Montreal offering three prizes for the best Canadian patriotic song to be sung at their Halloween rally. The story goes that soon after, he was walking along Laing Avenue when a maple leaf fell from a tree and clung to his overcoat. Five hours later, Muir had written "The Maple Leaf Forever". The song won the second prize of $50 for the young teacher and soon became Canada's unofficial national anthem. Soon afterwards, it was suggested to Muir that his song should be published. Taking his copy of the music to the Guardian newspaper office, he had a thousand copies run off. He sold $4 worth, then got a bill from the printer for $30. Thus, the first printing of "The Maple Leaf Forever" cost Alexander Muir $26.

Today the rousing song is seldom heard. Muir went on to become principal of Gladstone Public School which was renamed Alexander Muir Public School soon after the composer's death, which occurred on June 26, 1906 at his residence, 60 Churchill Avenue.

 # Daniel Lamb

## # 125, plot X, lot 50

*D*aniel Lamb's father Peter Lamb, emigrated to Upper Canada from England in 1834 and settled in Orillia. A few years later Peter and his young wife moved to Toronto and Lamb established a blacking and glue manufacturing factory just west of the Don Valley near the end of today's Winchester Street.

In 1842, a son Daniel was born and after attending school, took over his father's business which he ran, until the second of two serious fires destroyed the factory complex for good in 1888. Daniel Lamb is better remembered, however for his years as a member of City Council. He was first elected in 1885 and served almost continuously until 1901. During his 1893-1896 stint on Council, Lamb was Chairman of the Works Committee and in that capacity he was responsible for the establishment of the Riverdale Zoo, the building of Rosedale Drive (now Rosedale Valley Road), the reclamation of Ashbridge's Bay and the construction of the Island water filtration plant. Daniel Lamb died at his home, 156 Winchester Street, on August 26, 1920.

# James Cox Aikins

#126, plot V, lot 2

*B*orn in the Township of Toronto on March 30, 1823, young Aikins was educated in the local schools and then at Victoria College which was at that time still located in Cobourg, Ontario. He received his law degree, but decided that he'd rather be a farmer, at least until 1854 when he represented the County of Peel in the Legislative Assembly. Defeated in the general election of 1861, he returned the following year to represent the Home District, a position he held until Canadian Confederation in 1867. He was then appointed to the Senate, but he soon retired from that position to assume the post of Lieutenant Governor of Manitoba.

In 1869, he returned to a life of politics and served under Sir John A.Macdonald as Secretary of State until Macdonald's defeat in 1873. With the re-election of the Conservative Party in 1878, Aikins again served as Secretary of State, holding the position until 1880 when he became Minister of Inland Revenue. Resigning from the Cabinet in 1882, Aikins was again appointed Lieutenant Governor of Manitoba and and the District of Keewatin.

Following the expiration of his term in office, Aikins returned to Toronto where he took up residence at 29 Wellesley Street East and in 1894 was appointed a trustee of the Toronto General Burial Grounds (now Toronto Trust Cemeteries), a position he held until 1904. James Cox Aikins died at his Wellesley Street home on August 6, 1904.

# Rev. Henry John Cody

#127, plot V, lot 6

*B*orn in Embro, Ontario on December 6, 1868, Cody's ambition as a young man was to teach. But after three years on the staff of Ridley College in St. Catharines, he had a change of heart and decided instead to enter the ministry. Even before being ordained, Cody was assigned to a little church up in the Yorkville part of the city, where he and his sermons became so popular that within a few years of his arrival the church's seemingly insurmountable financial problems were healed with enough money left over to erect a beautiful new building on the south side of Bloor Street, just east of the "little Yorkville church" and west of the Jarvis Street corner. Cody remained rector of St. Paul's Anglican Church until his retirement in 1932, a total of thirty-three years. During that

time, he had the distinction of being one of the few non-bishop members of the clergy to preach before the King and Queen in Buckingham Palace.

Cody was elected to the Provincial Parliament and, in 1918, became the provincial Minister of Education. During his short stint in that position he was responsible for elevating the mandatory school age to sixteen. Cody also served as Chancellor, President and on the Board of Governors of the University of Toronto, served on the Board of Trustees of the Royal Ontario Museum, Toronto General Hospital and Wycliffe College, the school from which he had graduated many years before. He also held numerous other posts and directorships. Cody also helped found both Ridley and Havergal Colleges. The Hon. and Rev. Henry John Cody died on April 27, 1951.

Also buried in the Cody family plot is Henry Maurice Cody, who was drowned in a canoeing accident on the Marten River in northern Ontario on July 15, 1927. Maurice, as he was known to his friends, had attended the University of Toronto and was called to the bar in 1924. He was thirty years old and had been on a fishing holiday with a friend. They were accompanied by a guide and while the friend survived the accident, their twenty-year-old guide also drowned. The funeral for Maurice Cody was held at St. Paul's on July 18, 1927. Lieutenant Governor Ross and Ontario Premier Ferguson were in attendance. The St. Paul's church hall and a city public school were named in tribute to the young man.

# Byron Edmund Walker

### # 128, plot N, lot 4

*B*orn in the Township of Seneca in the Ontario County of Haldimand on October 14, 1858, Walker attended public school until the age of thirteen, when he quit to enter his uncle's private banking business in Hamilton. Seven years later, he joined a Hamilton branch of the Canadian Bank of Commerce as a discount clerk. Walker worked his way through the organization and in 1886 was appointed General Manager. A little more than twenty years later, he was bank President.

Walker is best remembered for his public activities which were legendary. He was a Trustee, Senator, Chairman and later Chancellor of the University of Toronto (which he helped re-organize in 1905-06), President of the Toronto Guild of Civic

Art, President of the federal commission to select works for the National Gallery and honourary President of the famous Mendelssohn Choir. Walker was an enthusiastic supporter of the Art Gallery of Toronto (now Ontario) and the Royal Ontario Museum, both institutions obtaining generous donations of money and material gifts on his death. He was also the founder and benefactor of the Champlain Society. Walker's directorships were numerous as were the titles of his various published works. In 1910, he was knighted by King George V.

Sir Byron Edmund Walker died at his residence Long Garth, 99 St.George Street, on March 27, 1924. An impressive funeral service was held in Convocation Hall the following day before an immense crowd, after which the body was borne to Mount Pleasant Cemetery for burial.

 # Frederick Burton Robins

#129, plot 7, lot 1

*B*orn in Stroud, Ontario, Robins came to Toronto as a youth and worked for a time in a law office before entering the real estate business in 1885. Twenty-three years later, he started his own company called Robins, Limited and at various times sold Toronto properties through offices he had set up in London, England and Glasgow, Scotland as well as in Detroit, Michigan. Robins subdivided many farms and estates in and around Toronto,

*Newspaper ad, 1914*

laid out thoroughfares and sold lots creating areas that have become well-established neighbourhood communities. For a period of time, Robins lived in a stately residence he called Strathrobyn, now the Canadian Forces Staff College at Wilson Avenue and Yonge Boulevard. The Duke of Windsor was his house guest during the Prince's visit to Canada in 1924. Frederick Robins died at the Wellesley Hospital on October 18, 1948.

# Charles Edward Goad

### # 130, plot 7, lot 5

*B*orn and educated in civil engineering in London, England, eighteen-year-old Charles Goad came to Canada in 1860 and entered the railway construction business. In 1876, he was appointed Chief Engineer of the Halifax and Cape Breton

205

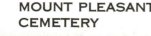

Railway. Six years later, Goad founded a publication known as the Insurance and Financial Chronicle in Montreal. Today, he is best known to historians for his Goad's Atlases, an invaluable series of fire insurance plans that outline in minute detail the construction materials, window and door locations etc. of virtually every structure in every major Canadian city. Goad died at his St. George Street residence on June 10, 1910.

# Lloyd Soules

## # 131, plot 6, sec 72, lot 5

*T*he sun shone brightly on the afternoon of August 10, 1914, as the small boat in which Mrs. Soules was sitting began drifting away from the Port McNicol shoreline, and further and further into Georgian Bay. Her daughter, eighteen-year-old Della Soules and her girlfriend, seventeen-year-old Edna Clarke swam desperately out into the bay in an attempt to retrieve the craft. Overcome by the cold water, the two girls soon began to panic. On shore, twenty-three-year-old Lloyd Soules saw their predicament and swam after them. As the horrified mother watched helplessly, all three young people were drowned beneath the unforgiving waters of Georgian Bay. Mrs. Soules was eventually rescued by neighbours. Friends to the sorrowful end, all three Lloyd, Della and Edna are buried in Mount Pleasant Cemetery.

# Martha Waites

#### # 132, plot 6, sec 76, lot 4

**W**hen the mighty Cunard liner *Lusitania* was sunk by a German submarine off the coast of Ireland on May 7, 1915, out of a passenger and crew manifest of 2,765, only 764 survived. In all, 2,001 men, women and children were killed. Thirty-nine-year-old Martha Waites of 53 1/2 Olive Avenue was one of the ninety-eight passengers from Toronto who perished in the cold waters of the Atlantic Ocean. Her fellow passenger A.R. Clarke (PLOT 1, LOT 3 & 10) survived the sinking, only to die a few weeks later from complications arising from pneumonia that he contracted while in the cold water.

# Sarah Sloan

#### # 133, plot 7, sec 24, lot 12

**O**n the afternoon of July 7, 1915 picnickers from two Toronto churches, Woodgreen Methodist on Queen Street East and St. John's Presbyterian on Broadview Avenue were enjoying a summer outing at Queenston, Ontario. Some had decided to climb to the top of the Brock Monument on the Heights overlooking the pretty little village on the banks of the Niagara River. Suddenly it began to rain and many picnickers scrambled aboard the small open-sided streetcar that zigzagged its way from Queen-

ston Heights down to the covered lake boat wharf. Badly overloaded, the car started its slow descent. But the excess weight and slick track proved too much and soon the car was racing down the steep embankment out of control. Half way down the hill, the track curved. Even on a clear, dry day the turn was always approached with caution, but this time, as the operator fought to regain control, the car lurched at the curve, came off the tracks and crashed full speed into a huge tree. Of the approximately 150 passengers that had squeezed onto streetcar number 685, 120 were injured in the crash while a total of fifteen were killed outright or hurt so badly that they succumbed to their injuries before the lake boat transporting them back to Toronto hospitals for treatment could complete the crossing. Fifty-three-year-old Sarah Sloan was one of victims who died aboard the Niagara steamer *Chippewa*. Two other victims are also buried in Mount Pleasant Cemetery, Charles Jennings (PLOT X, SECT 9, LOT 17) and Harold Partridge (PLOT H, SEC 9, LOT 8).

 # Oliver Mowat

## # 134, plot W, lot 57

*A* native of Kingston, Ontario, where the future Premier of Ontario and Father of Confederation was born on July 22, 1820, Mowat attended the Kingston Grammar School and went on to study law, being called to the bar in 1842. After practicing in his hometown for a short period, Mowat left for Toronto where he entered into a partnership with Messrs Burns and VanKoughnet.

In 1857, Mowat was elected Alderman for the city's St. Lawrence Ward, a position he held for St. James Ward the following year. During 1857, Mowat was elected to the Legislative Assembly and in 1864 was a delegate to the conference on the Confederation of Canada held that year in Quebec City. He took an active part in preparing the Constitutional Act of Confederation, thus becoming one of the true Fathers of Confederation. In 1872, Mowat accepted the position of Premier and Attorney-General of the Province of Ontario and retained the premiership until 1896 when he was elected an M.P. in the government of Prime Minister Wilfrid Laurier. Sir Oliver Mowat received his knighthood in 1892. The year after he was appointed to the Canadian Senate, Mowat was chosen to be Ontario's eighth Lieutenant Governor on November 18, 1897. He died on April 19, 1903.

# Newton Wesley Rowell

# 135, plot W, lot 42

*B*orn in Middlesex County, Ontario on November 1, 1867, Rowell was educated in the local public and high school system after which he began his law studies in London, Ontario. He completed his degree at Toronto's Osgoode Hall and was called to the bar in 1891. Nine years later, Rowell ran as a Liberal for the Provincial Parliament, only to be defeated. He tried again in 1911 and this time was successful holding the North Oxford riding for the next six years, during which period he was also Leader of the Provincial Liberal Party. In 1917, Rowell entered federal politics and held several important positions during his three-and-a-half year tenure as M.P. for the riding of Durham, including a place on the extremely influential Imperial War Cabinet. In 1919, he was Canadian delegate to the congress in Washington that established the League of Nations and became one of this new organization's most ardent supporter.

In 1936, at the age of seventy, Rowell was appointed Chief Justice of Ontario and in the following year, chaired a royal commission that studied the state of Canadian Confederation, seventy years after the original four provinces had first joined together on July 1, 1867. He was a Governor of the University of Toronto and Vice-Chancellor of Victoria College. Rowell suffered a severe heart attack in 1938 and remained confined to his residence for the last years of his life, passing away on November 22, 1941.

# Edward Leadlay

## # 136, plot V, lot 47

**B**orn in Scarborough, England in 1827, Edward Leadlay obtained his education in his hometown and then entered the milling business. He then emigrated to Dundee in the State of New York, where he continued to work in the milling business for several more years before moving across the lake and settling in Toronto in 1863. Leadlay helped establish the Standard Woolen Mills and also entered into the leather and sheepskin business with stores on Queen Street at Crawford and at 87 Front Street East. He was also a senior director of the Dominion Bank. In 1876, Leadlay built a beautiful residence at 25 Esther (now Augusta) Street that is now used by the Felician Sisters as a school. In was in this house that Edward Leadlay died on September 17, 1899.

# Archibald Douglas

## # 137, plot V, lot Y

**A** few miles east of Sarnia, Ontario is the small hamlet of Wanstead. On the night of December 26, 1902, the speeding westbound Grand Trunk Pacific Express, running an hour-and-a-half late, collided head-on with a slow moving eastbound freight, resulting in the death of twenty-five passengers including Archibald Douglas.

**MOUNT PLEASANT CEMETERY**

# Arthur Godfrey Peuchen

#138, plot V, lot 58

*B*orn in Montreal on April 18, 1859, Peuchen was educated in several of the city's private schools. With an interest in forestry and chemistry, Peuchen became the first person in the British Empire to make acetone directly from wood. Acetone was an important constituent of the explosive cordite and, as such, was much sought after by the British Government. In 1897, Peuchen and William Mackenzie organized the Standard Chemical Company to manufacture acetone in large quantities. The company owned and operated lumber mills, factories and refineries throughout Ontario and Quebec, with additional refineries in England, France and Germany. With business interests on both sides of the Atlantic, Peuchen crossed the Atlantic on numerous occasions.

For his return trip from England in the early spring of 1912, bought a first-class ticket for several thousand dollars on the maiden trip of the White Star Line's wondrous new liner *R.M.S. Titanic*. When the ill-fated craft struck an iceberg late in the evening of April 14, Peuchen, who was a talented yachtsman and active member of Toronto's Royal Canadian Yacht Club, was given command of lifeboat number six. Under his leadership, almost a dozen people in the boat, including the legendary "unsinkable" Molly Brown, were eventually rescued by the Cunard liner Carpathia.

Peuchen testified before the American commission on the *Titanic* tragedy in which 1,513 were lost out of a total passenger and crew manifest of 2,224. Following his return to Toronto, where for a short time he was regarded as a hero, Peuchen soon became the victim of a questioning public. "Why had he survived when so many women and children perished?" Unable to stand the pressures placed on him, Peuchen retired and moved to Alberta. He died at the age of seventy on December 7, 1929.

 # Marion Martin

## # 139, plot V, lot A

On March 13, 1876, fifty-year-old Scottish-born Marion Martin, who had died two days earlier, was interred in Plot P, Section 3, Lot 1. Hers was the very first burial in Mount Pleasant Cemetery. On October 22, 1891, her remains were removed to the Martin family plot where she now rests.

**MOUNT PLEASANT CEMETERY**

# George William Ross

## # 140, plot V, lot R

*B*orn near the community of Nairn in the County of Middlesex, Ontario on September 18, 1841 George Ross was educated in the local schools before coming to Toronto and obtaining his teaching certificate at the Normal School. He then attended Albert University in Belleville, graduating with an honours LL.D. After being a teacher and inspector of public schools in western Ontario for some years, he returned to college, obtained a law degree and was called to the bar in 1887.

Politically, Ross sat in the House of Commons from 1872 until 1883 when he resigned to run provincially, becoming the Minister of Education in the Mowat (PLOT W, LOT 58) administration. Of particular interest to Torontonians is the fact that in 1887 it was Ross who introduced legislation to authorize the federation of the University of Toronto and the affiliation of the denominational colleges with that national institution. In 1899, Ross became the Premier of Ontario until his defeat and retirement from office in the provincial election of 1905. He continued as leader of the Opposition Party until called to the Senate of Canada in 1907. Three years later, Ross was knighted by King George V. In the business world he was, at various times, a Director of Union Trust and the Globe Printing Company, President of Manufacturers Life Insurance Company. George William Ross died at his residence, 3 Elmsley Place, on March 7, 1914.

# Robert Simpson
## # 141, plot V, lot 153

*B*orn and educated in Speymouth, Scotland, Simpson received an early apprenticeship in the dry goods business before emigrating to Upper Canada in 1854 at the age of twenty. He obtained employment in a general store in Newmarket, opening his own store in partnership with William Trent four years later. In 1862, Simpson's business was destroyed by fire and, though he rebuilt, two years later another conflagration ravaged the Simpson store. Again the young Scot rebuilt and again fire struck. This time, insurance was unable to cover the losses and Simpson's creditors had to settle for one-third of what they were owed. Not long after, Simpson sold his Newmarket interests and moved to Toronto where, sometime during the winter of 1872-73, he opened a small dry goods store at 184 Yonge Street, a few doors north of Queen Street.

Business prospered and in 1881, Simpson moved to larger premises at 174-76 Yonge Street, south of Queen and adjacent to a store owned by an Irishman by the name of Timothy Eaton (PLOT 2, LOT 4). (Interestingly, in 1883 Eaton moved to a new location north of Queen Street, but recognizing the competition the Simpson business posed, kept his old store padlocked for months so Simpson couldn't expand into it.) Simpson's business continued to flourish and in 1890, he entered into partnership with his brother James and James Robertson. Together the trio opened a wholesale and retail dry goods operation on Colborne Street under the name Simpson, Robertson and Simpson. Following the death of his brother, the business was sold and Robert focussed all of his attention on his Yonge Street retail outlet.

In 1893, he erected a handsome new six-storey structure at the very busy southwest corner of Yonge and Queen Streets to the plans of architect Edmund Burke (PLOT S, LOT D). But again fire was his nemesis and in March of 1895, the store was gutted in one of three fires that inflicted heavy damage on the city's core in the early months of that year. Undaunted, the following year Simpson rebuilt an updated and improved version of the 1894 structure, a building that still forms the cornerstone of the present-day Simpson's downtown business.

On December 14, 1897, Robert Simpson died suddenly at his Bloor Street East residence at the relatively young age of sixty-three. With no male heir to whom the business could be handed, the Simpson enterprise with its 500 employees serving in thirty-five departments, was sold for $135,000 to a syndicate of three prominent businessmen, Harris Henry Fudger, Joseph Flavelle (TRIANGLE 26) and Albert Ernest Ames (PLOT 2, LOT 8).

# Arthur Hewitt

## # 142, plot V, lot 132

*W*hen their small boat was overturned late in the afternoon of June 11, 1911 in a violent squall off Lorne Park, a small summer cottage community on the shores of Lake Ontario a few miles west of Toronto, eighteen-year-old St. Andrew's College student Arthur Hewitt placed his two younger companions on top of their capsized dinghy and swam to get help. As he swam towards shore, the heavy swells caused by the storm were too much for Arthur Hewitt. His powerful strokes slowed and soon Hewitt slipped beneath the waves and drowned. The other boys, ages ten and thirteen, were eventually saved. The marker on the young man's grave is inscribed with the words "GAVE HIS LIFE TO SAVE OTHERS".

# David Alexander Dunlap

## # 143, plot V, lot 124

*D*avid Dunlap was born in Pembroke, Ontario in 1862 and received his public and high school education in that community. He furthered his studies in Barrie, Ontario and Toronto where he graduated with a law degree from Osgoode Hall. He then

**MOUNT PLEASANT CEMETERY**

moved to Mattawa, Ontario and set up his legal practice. But his heart was in prospecting and he soon became involved with the Timmins Brothers, also residents of Mattawa. Together, the trio established what became the very successful La Rose Mine near Cobalt. A few years later, he invested in mines in the Porcupine area and helping create the Hollinger Consolidated project.

Though extremely wealthy, Dunlap was also a great benefactor donating thousands to the University of Toronto, St. Andrew's College, the Methodist Church of Canada and the Royal Ontario Museum. Dunlap had also maintained a 600-acre country summer retreat which he called Don Alda Farm after his wife's middle name (now the Donalda Golf Course and club house situated southwest of the York Mills Road-Don Valley Parkway interchange). With its unmatched dairy herd and poultry stock, the farm was one of the most modern and efficient farm complexes on the continent.

It was at the farm that David Alexander Dunlap died on October 29, 1924 at the age of sixty-one. The funeral was conducted at his city residence, 93 Highland Avenue in Rosedale. Also buried in the family plot is Dunlap's wife, Jessie Donalda Dunlap. In 1930, Mrs. Dunlap announced that she would be presenting to the University of Toronto an observatory on Yonge Street just south of Richmond Hill in memory of her late husband and his keen interest in astronomy. The David Dunlap Observatory opened in 1935. Jessie Dunlap died at her Highland Avenue home on July 31, 1946.

 # John Irvine Davidson

## # 144, plot V, lot 126

*B*orn in Scotland on November 17, 1854, Davidson came to Toronto as a young man. He established himself in the wholesale grocery business with John Hay, under the name of Davidson and Hay. He held various business directorships and participated in the community's military life, first as a Second Lieutenant in the Royal Grenadiers, retiring from that organization with the rank of Captain in 1890.

In October of the following year, the 48th Regiment (Highlanders) was formed and Davidson was selected as its first commanding officer. In tribute to Davidson, the new regiment agreed to adopt both the Davidson tartan and family crest which continue to be revered by members of the 48th Highlanders to this day. Davidson remained the unit's commanding officer until March 16, 1898, when he stepped down.

He remained active in both the business and military endeavors until he took ill in the spring of 1909. On April 28, 1910, the fifty-six year old Davidson succumbed to cancer at his residence, 158 St. George Street, and was given a full military burial at Mount Pleasant Cemetery on April 30, following a brief service at St. Andrew's Presbyterian Church on King Street West. It was recorded in the daily newspapers that the funeral cortege, complete with gun carriage and full representation by members of the city's various military units, was one of the largest in Toronto history. A beautiful memorial to those members of the 48th Highlanders who gave their lives to keep our country free was originally erected near the

219

**MOUNT PLEASANT CEMETERY**

Davidson plot. It was moved in 1969 to a more conspicuous location, just inside the cemetery gates on the east side of Mount Pleasant Road.

 # Robert Clifford Darling
## # 145, plot V, lot 89

*M*ore than 6,000 Canadian troops were killed in the defence of Ypres in Belgium during the First World War. During this battle, twenty-seven-year-old Captain Robert Darling of the 48th Highlanders was seriously wounded when a bullet pierced a main artery. On March 23, 1915, he was evacuated to the military hospital in Amesbury, England. Less than a month later, on April 19, 1915, the young Torontonian died. His body was returned to his hometown and on May 6, 1915, after a private service at the family home, 2 Dale Avenue in Rosedale and public funeral at St. James' Square Presbyterian Church, Darling was buried in a plot in Mount Pleasant Cemetery. This plot was specially selected because of its proximity to the graves of other fallen Highlanders and to that of Col. Davidson, the unit's first commanding officer (PLOT V, LOT 126). Unlike the long standing tradition of burying military casualties near where they fell, Captain Darling was the first Canadian soldier in history to die on foreign soil and subsequently returned to Canada for burial.

# Joseph Wesley Flavelle

### # 146, triangle 26

**B**orn in Peterborough, Ontario on February 15, 1858, young Flavelle entered the local school system, but quit when he was just thirteen. He worked for a time in the flour and feed business in his hometown for a time, then moved to Toronto in 1887 where he became associated with William Davies, the meat packer. He helped turn a mediocre operation into one of the most efficient and prosperous on the continent.

During the First World War, Flavelle was appointed to the important and powerful position of Chairman of the Imperial Munitions Board, an organization responsible for all shell production. In short order, he managed to turn around an organization that was both ineffectual and inefficient into an operation that was well organized and run and did much to secure victory for the Allies. In 1917, Flavelle was knighted for his efforts. Unfortunately, later in the war Flavelle's reputation was

**MOUNT PLEASANT
CEMETERY**

tarnished when he was accused of profiteering by selling the military "tainted" bacon. He was completely exonerated by a special committee and in spite of this cloud over his head, he continued to be member of numerous public bodies including the Royal Ontario Museum, Toronto General Hospital and the University of Toronto and was always held in the highest esteem by his peers. He was almost single-handedly responsible for the establishment of the Ontario Research Foundation.

In the winter of 1939, while enjoying his traditional Florida winter holiday, Sir Joseph Flavelle was suddenly stricken at his Palm Beach home and died on March 7, 1939, at the age of eighty-one. His remains were returned to his Toronto residence called Holwood, one of the few residences still standing on Queen's Park. Here a private service was held prior to a public funeral at Sherbourne Street United Church on the following Saturday, March 11. Burial followed in the family's unique underground vault, (built in 1932) at Mount Pleasant Cemetery. Also interred in the vault are Lady Flavelle (d.1932), the couple's seven-month-old daughter Josephine (d.1888), daughters Clara (d.1966) and Mina (d.1971) and son Sir Ellsworth Flavelle (d.1977). At his death, Flavelle's estate totalled over $6 million (1939).

 # John Reginald Thorne

## # 147, plot Y, lot 121

*B*orn in Toronto in 1890 and educated at the Technical High School on College Street, Reginald Thorne was the son of Major J. O. Thorne of the

Queen's Own Rifles. On the evening of June 20, 1910, a military pageant was held at the Exhibition Grandstand during which Reginald Thorne, a private with his father's regiment was to portray Joseph Sheppard sitting astride a horse while another member of the regiment portrayed the fiery Scot William Lyon Mackenzie exhorting his companions to attack the City of Toronto. At one point in the scene, as the rebels were being routed by the Loyalists, a volley of rifle fire caused Thorne's mount to rear up and fall backwards full-length on the young soldier who was still astride his mount. Thorne was impaled by the pommel on the saddle. The young man was taken to the hospital where his injuries were diagnosed as non-life threatening. Later the next day, July 21, 1910, twenty-year-old John Reginald Thorne died of internal injuries and heart failure. The young soldier's unexpected demise can be deduced from words he uttered as he was taken from the grandstand, words that have been immortalized on his memorial stone: "TELL MOTHER I'LL BE ALL RIGHT IN THE MORNING".

# John Croft

## # 148, plot P, lot 2242

*A* month after the heart of Toronto was devastated by fire, forty-year-old John Croft was busily dynamiting what was left standing of some of the structures on Front Street West. Croft had gained experience with dynamite while he was a young man working in the mines in his native England and was quick to volunteer when the city fathers

**MOUNT PLEASANT
CEMETERY**

needed someone to help them get the city back on its feet. Spring was in the air that May fourth morning back in 1904, but the smell of so many burned out buildings made its presence hard to notice in downtown Toronto. Working on Front Street just east of Bay, John Croft had just inserted three sticks of dynamite in a narrow crevice at the base of the teetering south wall of the W. J. Gage Building, 54-58 Front Street West, and lit the fuse. Several bobby-helmeted policemen kept the inquisitive crowds back, while Croft ran for cover. Shortly, two thuds reverberated throughout the area and the wall began to sway. Several minutes went by, but there was no third detonation. Croft waited a few more minutes then went to see what had happened. As he examined the "dud" stick, it suddenly exploded in the young man's face. He was horribly maimed and quickly removed to the Emergency Hospital just up Bay Street. First reports suggested that although he was in serious condition, Croft would probably survive.

Ten hours later, that prediction was suddenly changed and the family was summoned. At nine-fifty in the morning, May 5, 1904, the Great Toronto Fire had claimed its first, and thankfully only victim. Two days later, Croft's wife and their three children silently wept as John Croft was laid to rest in a simple grave in Mount Pleasant Cemetery.

# George Pears

#149, plot P, lot 1

*A* native of Yorkshire, England, Pears came to Toronto as a young man in 1851 with his brother

Leonard. George Pears established the area's first coffee and spice mills called the Western Canada Coffee and Spice Mills. The enterprise was located at the northeast corner of Yonge and Alexander Streets, while Pears himself resided nearby at 15 Grosvenor Street. George Pears retired from the business in the mid-1880s and embarked on a second career in real estate at which he was also very successful.

Pears died on April 22, 1913 and is interred in the Pears' mausoleum along with his wife Dedamia (d.1910), two sons, Edward (d.1915) and George Jr. (d.1918), three daughters Emily (d.1925), Alice (d.1942) and Florence (d.1944), and Florence's husband John Buchanan (d.1930). Interred in the surrounding lot are six other family members.

 # Alexander Rogers

**# 150, triangle 11**

**W**e know little about the early life of Alexander Rogers, other than that he was born in Toronto in 1835 and attended both the Normal School and Upper Canada College, then on King Street West. In 1884, he embarked on a career in the wholesale tobacco business. His first warehouse was in a small building at 42 Adelaide Street West, which was eventually vacated for larger premises at 151 Queen Street West. Alexander Rogers died at his residence, 177 Simcoe Street, on May 29, 1912, at the age of seventy-seven. At present, ten people are interred in the Rogers' mausoleum.

# Austin Mitchell

# 151, plot 12, sec 2, lot 15

**B**orn in Alliston, Ontario in 1875, Mitchell joined the Toronto Police Force in 1899. He was promoted to the rank of detective in 1910, and some years later was assigned to the famous Ambrose Small case. Millionaire theatre-magnate Ambrose Small disappeared on the afternoon of December 2, 1919, after selling the major part of his theatrical empire, including Toronto's Grand Opera House on Adelaide Street West. Detective Mitchell was entangled in the Small case twenty-four hours a day for years and, while the leads took him far and wide, Mitchell was unable to come up with a solution. The Ambrose Small case remains unsolved to this day. Austin Mitchell died on January 4, 1950.

# George W. Gouinlock

# 152, plot 10, lot 37

**B**orn in Paris, Ontario, Gouinlock received much of his later education in Winnipeg, coming to Toronto around the turn-of-the-century, where he practiced his architectural skills for more than thirty years. He was responsible for such diverse Toronto landmarks as the Alexandra Palace apartment building on University Avenue and the Temple Building at the northwest corner of Richmond and Bay Streets, both of which have been

226

Agricultural or Province Building, Toronto Exhibition, Canada

*Gouinlock's Horticultural Building at the Canadian National Exhibition, c.1910.*

demolished. Several Gouinlock-designed structures, the Administration Building (1905) (now Press Building), Horticulture Building (1907), Music Building (1908) and British Government Building (1912) (now Arts, Crafts and Hobbies Building) still stand in the Exhibition grounds. George Gouinlock died on February 13, 1932.

# William Mackenzie
## # 153, plot 10, lot 27

*L*ate in the afternoon of April 23, 1929, twenty-seven-year-old William Mackenzie was at the controls of the Toronto Flying Club's Moth biplane G-CAVF, when it lost power shortly after take-off from the Leaside airfield near the corner of today's busy Eglinton Avenue/Laird Drive intersection and

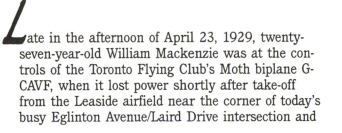

crashed. Both the pilot and his young student Noel Marshall (PLOT L, LOT 34, SEC 13) were killed in the accident, the first tragedy to befall the recently organized flying club. Ironically, Mackenzie was the nephew of Count Jacques de Lesseps who, in 1911, was the first person to fly an aircraft over Toronto. He too was killed in a plane crash near Gaspe in 1928.

 # John A. Pearson
## # 154, plot 10, lot 20

*B*orn in Derbyshire, England on June 22, 1867, Pearson came to Toronto in 1888, and two years later joined with Frank Darling to form the architectural firm of Darling and Pearson. One of their first commissions was to design structures to replace those destroyed in the great St. John's, Newfoundland conflagration of 1892. The firm of Darling and Pearson designed many other notable Canadian landmarks, including the Sun Life Building in Montreal and the main block of the Parliament Buildings in Ottawa after the original block had been destroyed by fire in 1916. Toronto landmarks attributed to the team of Darling and Pearson include the C.P.R. and Dominion Bank Buildings at the southeast and southwest corners, respectively, of Yonge and King Streets, the Mount Pleasant Mausoleum, the Toronto General Hospital on College Street, the University of Toronto's Convocation and Simcoe Halls, the Canadian Bank of Commerce on King Street West. When construction of this latter building now called Commerce Court North was completed, it was the tallest building in the Commonwealth. It is now called Commerce Court North. In 1935, Pearson retired from active architectural work though he remained active with the Ontario Association of Architects. John Pearson died at his residence, 210 Forest Hill Road, on June 11, 1940.

# Henry DePencier
### # 155, plot 10, lot 198

*B*orn in Wakefield, Quebec, DePencier joined Rand Mines in Johannesburg, South Africa in 1903. He became Vice-President and General Manager of Dome Mines Limited which had gone into the gold mining business in the Porcupine area of Northern Ontario in 1910. DePencier died in New York City on November 29, 1935.

# Clifford Sifton
### # 156, plot 10, lot 201

*B*orn in Middlesex County, Ontario on March 10, 1861, Clifford Sifton was educated in the public schools of London, Ontario and Victoria College, Cobourg. He was called to the bar of Manitoba in 1882. Sifton entered the world of politics in 1888

and was elected to the Manitoba Legislature eventually becoming Attorney-General and then Minister of Education. In 1898, he was elected to the Federal Government representing the riding of Brandon, Manitoba, a position he held until 1911 when he resigned from active political life over a dispute he had with the leadership who were advocating "free trade" with the United States. During Sifton's tenure as federal Minister of the Interior, he campaigned vigorously for increased American, British and European immigration to help settle the vast Canadian west. Sifton was also responsible for the satisfactory negotiation of the Crow's Nest Pass agreement with the C.P.R., the administration of the Yukon during the gold rush and in 1903 was appointed as the Canadian representative on the Alaskan Boundary Tribunal. He was knighted by King George V in 1915.

In the business world, Sifton was President of the Atlantic Oil Company, Managing Director of the Imperial Pulp Company and later owned several newspapers including the *Manitoba Free Press*. He was also a lover of fine horses. Following his retirement from politics, Sifton moved to Toronto and built a large residence on Lawrence Avenue East which he called Armadale. It is now the home of the Toronto French School. Sir Clifford Sifton died while visiting a medical specialist in New York City on April 16, 1929. Interment followed three days later.

 # James Henry Gundy

## # 157, plot 10, lot 110

*A* native of Harriston, Ontario, Gundy was born the son of a Methodist Minister on March 22, 1880. He received his early education in London and Windsor, Ontario, coming to Toronto at the age of eighteen, where he joined the Central Canada Loan and Savings Company. When Dominion Securities Corporation was established in 1900, Gundy was appointed secretary.

It was while he was with Dominion Securities that he and co-worker George Herbert Wood decided to strike out on their own, establishing Wood, Gundy and Company in 1905. In addition to guiding the Wood, Gundy firm to the forefront of Canadian financial investment institutions, Gundy also sat as a director on the boards of numerous other companies and acted as a financial advisor to the Federal Government during both war and

peacetime. Following the end of the Second World War, it was the Wood, Gundy organization that was responsible for raising the huge amount of capital required by Ontario Hydro as it strove to meet the province's electrical needs in the post-war boom period.

James Gundy died on November 10, 1951 at the age of seventy-one. At his death, Gundy owned a large parcel of land adjacent to the Don River in the Town of Leaside. The property which now comprises Serena Gundy Park in North York was donated by Gundy in honour of his first wife Serena Lake Clark, who predeceased him by ten years and is also buried in the Gundy plot.

# William Howard Hearst

# 158, plot 10, lot 97

On February 15, 1864, William Howard Hearst was born in the Arran Township in the Ontario County of Bruce. He attended both public and high school in Collingwood and then law school at Osgoode Hall in Toronto, being called to the bar in 1888. Ten years later he was elected M.P.P. for Sault Ste. Marie. When the Hon. Frank Cochrane entered federal politics in 1911, Hearst was made Minister of Lands and Forests. A short time later, when the Premier of Ontario Sir James Whitney died, Hearst was appointed Leader of the party and assumed the premiership on October 2, 1914, a position he held for five years. During his tenure,

his two most important legislative enactments were the enfranchisement of women and the passing of the Ontario Temperance Act which led to eleven years of prohibition. Hearst was also instrumental in ensuring that the massive Queenston-Chippewa hydro-electric power development was realized. He was knighted on February 13, 1917. On September 29, 1941, Sir William Hearst, Ontario's seventh Premier, died at his residence, 80 Glen Road in Rosedale. The Town of Hearst in northern Ontario, formerly called the Town of Grant, was renamed in honour of this distinguished politician.

# Lawrence Solman
## # 159, plot 10, lot 90

*L*awrence (Lol) Solman was born in Toronto on May 14, 1863 and educated in the city's public schools, before attending the Mechanic's Institute on Church Street. As a young man, he opened a mail order business in Detroit which he operated for ten years, before returning to Toronto and marrying Emily Hanlan, sister of the great sculler Ned Hanlan. As a member of the prominent Toronto Island family, Solman became interested in the development of an amusement park and sports complex at Hanlan's Point. He started a ferry service which eventually evolved into the highly successful Toronto Ferry Company. When the company was purchased by the Toronto Transportation Commission many years later, it had a virtual monopoly on all Island-bound traffic.

*Toronto's Royal Alexandra Theatre, once managed by Lawrence Solman.*

Solman also acquired the popular International League Toronto Maple Leaf baseball team and was responsible for giving the team a new, modern grandstand at Hanlan's Point. The thousands of ball fans could only get there on his ferryboats *Blue Bell* and the recently restored *Trillium*. When the city appropriated the ferry fleet in 1926, Solman moved his team to a new stadium he had just built at the foot of Bathurst Street. In addition to his Island interests, Solman promoted the construction of the recently demolished Terrace (originally called the Arena Gardens) on Mutual Street and was Managing Director of the Royal Alexandra Theatre on King Street West for many years. He also managed Sunnyside Amusement Park and was a Vice-President of Loew's Canadian Theatres. Lawrence Solman died in Wellesley Hospital after a long illness on March 24, 1931 at the age of sixty-four.

 # Leonard Allan
## # 160, plot 9, lot 3253

*O*n September 1, 1919, five-month-old Leonard Allan died at Sick Children's Hospital on College Street. After a brief funeral service at the youngster's residence at 105 Trinity Street, friends and family went by motor hearse to Mount Pleasant Cemetery while the youngster's casket was taken to the foot of Bathurst Street, where it was strapped in front of the pilot of a Curtis biplane and flown to a field just east of the cemetery. From here, the casket was taken by hearse to the grave site.

**MOUNT PLEASANT CEMETERY**

When asked why this procedure was followed, Funeral Director Robert Stone stated that the day would come when aerial funerals would be common place. So it was that the funeral of little Leonard Allan was the first aerial funeral conducted anywhere in the world.

# Florence Robinson
## # 161, plot 8, lot 6192

*I*n the summer and fall of 1918, the world suffered the worst epidemic since the Black Death pandemic of the mid-fourteenth century. The "Spanish" influenza (which actually began in China, though it was in Spain that 80% of the population was affected) was first diagnosed on this side of the Atlantic Ocean in Boston on August 27. South of the border, more than half a million people died including 19,000 in New York City. In Ontario, almost three 300,000 were affected with more than 8,700 dying from its affects.

In Toronto, thirty-two-year-old Florence Robinson was typical of the hundreds that died locally. She passed away on October 24, 1918 and was buried three days later in PLOT 8 where many other influenza victims were interred.

A quick look at the Mt. Pleasant's interment book reveals that, on October 25, 1918 a total of eleven victims of the dreaded Spanish influenza were buried in the cemetery on that day alone.

# Gordon Tamblyn

## # 162, plot 10, lot 171

**B**orn in Bellwood, Ontario in 1878, the young Tamblyn attended school in Markham and then apprenticed with a Whitby druggist before attending the Ontario College of Pharmacy on Gerrard Street in Toronto. Having obtained his degree, Tamblyn worked in the Burgess-Powell Drug Store at 76 Yonge Street for a few years before investing a hard-earned $500 and opening the first drug store under the G. Tamblyn name, at the southeast corner of Queen Street and Lee Avenue in the Beach area of the city in 1904. Tamblyn lived a few doors down the street at 16 Lee Avenue. A few years later, after the Tamblyn chain had grown substantially, the entire operation was purchased by United Cigar Stores. They in turn, were purchased by the owners of the huge Imperial Tobacco empire. In 1929, Tamblyn, who had remained in constant control of the drug store part of the business, bought back his company, which by then had grown to forty stores and had yearly sales in excess of $4 million. On August 18, 1933 while playing the seventh hole at the Rosedale golf course, Tamblyn suffered a heart attack and died. In recent years, the Tamblyn chain was sold to Boots who then sold out to PharmaPlus.

# Mount Pleasant Road

*The new Mount Pleasant Road through the cemetery, c.1920.*

*I*n the beginning, the plot of land fronting on north Yonge Street in York Township that had been purchased by the Toronto General Burying Ground Trustees in 1873 as the site of their new cemetery, was nothing more than a large field liberally dotted with trees and interspersed with several fast flowing creeks.

The property ran from Yonge Street "projected" (which due to a surveyor's miscalculation is today's Lawton Boulevard) one-and-one-quarter miles east to the First Concession Road (now Bayview Avenue) and covered a total of 200-acres. The Yonge Street frontage was one-quarter mile.

As the communities to the north of the new cemetery began to develop, it soon became obvious that a new north-south road through the develop-

238

ing cemetery would make commuting into and out of the city to the south much more convenient. As the years passed, a pair of unconnected and unpaved roads, each called Mount Pleasant Road (because of their proximity to the cemetery) were laid out north and south of the cemetery property. They were quiet little back roads that led nowhere. When the City of Toronto annexed the fast-growing Town of North Toronto in 1912, that often talked-about thoroughfare through the cemetery grounds which had started out simply as a convenience to commuters soon became a genuine necessity.

As important as the road may have been to the city and the citizens of the north end, the cemetery Trustees continued to resist any attempts to bisect their property with a road of any kind, arguing that such a project would greatly lessen the value of Mount Pleasant Cemetery. It wasn't until March, 1915 that the city finally enacted By-law 7311 which authorize the construction of a road connecting the two existing Mount Pleasant Roads and empowered the city to expropriate the necessary right-of-way through the cemetery grounds.

*City workers lay streetcar track on the Mount Pleasant Road bridge over the Belt Line Railway, 1919.*

MOUNT PLEASANT
CEMETERY

With this hurdle cleared, the city started discussions with the Toronto General Burying Grounds Trust to ascertain an amount of money to compensate the trustees. In July, the newspapers reported that the city would pay the trustees the enormous sum of $98,921.88 for a right-of-way one-quarter mile in length and seventy-six feet in width. An additional $2,211.80 was added for "filling and cutting".

Work on the new thoroughfare started in the spring of 1917 and the unpaved road, complete with a humped-back bridge over the Belt Line Railway's old right-of-way (by now used as solely a freight line) was ready for traffic in 1919. Interestingly, the road over the bridge was paved and even had streetcar tracks in place. The stretch of new road through the cemetery connected with two small north-south roads to form today's Mount Pleasant Road running from St. Clair Avenue to Eglinton Avenue.

To coincide with the November opening of the T.T.C.'s new Mount Pleasant Road extension of the ST. CLAIR streetcar line north to a loop at Eglinton Avenue, the entire thoroughfare was paved in 1925.

*TTC crew lay track on Mount Pleasant Road, 1925.*

**AS YOU CROSS MOUNT PLEASANT ROAD TO CONTINUE YOUR TOUR OF THE CEMETERY PLEASE BE CAREFUL AND WATCH FOR THE TRAFFIC.**

# Donald Summerville

*B*orn in Toronto on August 4, 1915, Don Summerville was educated at Frankland Public School, Danforth Technical School and Shaw's Business College. His early employment was with his father, Billy Summerville who was a City Alderman and owned Danforth-Woodbine Theatres Limited and Summerville Properties. For a time, the younger Summerville managed the Prince of Wales Theatre on the Danforth.

In 1955, Summerville entered municipal politics as Alderman for Ward 8 a position he held until 1958. From 1959 through 1962 he was a City Controller and was elected Mayor in 1963, defeating long-time incumbent Nathan Phillips for the job. Early in the evening of November 19, 1963, Mayor Summerville made his way to the

**MOUNT PLEASANT CEMETERY**

George Bell Arena where he was to play in a charity hockey game with the proceeds going to the Italian Flood Relief Fund. Summerville had been a practice goalie with the Maple Leaf hockey team, so it was only natural that he would play that position on a team made up of City Council members. They were to play a team of City Hall press gallery members. After only a few minutes in the net, the mayor headed for the dressing room, and while sitting on the bench complained of not feeling well. Reaching for his coat pocket (and a bottle of nitroglycerine tablets that he kept close at hand ever since suffering a slight coronary in 1961), Summerville slumped to the floor and within moments the second Mayor in the city's history to die while in office had succumbed to a massive coronary occlusion. His father William Allan Summerville (d.1972) is also buried in this family plot.

 # 48th Highlanders' Memorial

## # 164, east of Mt. Pleasant road gate

*F*ormed in Toronto on October 16, 1891 with Captain John Irvine Davidson (see PLOT V, LOT 26) as the first commanding officer, the 48th Highlanders of Canada first saw active service in the South African War (1899-1902) when seventeen Highlanders accompanied the First Canadian contingent overseas. Following the death of Lieutenant-Colonel Davidson in April of 1910, the regiment purchased a large burial lot in Mount Pleasant Cemetery. Late in the afternoon of Thanksgiving Monday, October 28, 1912, the troop train bringing seven hundred troops back to the city from a sham bat-

tle that had been held that day near Milton,
Ontario crashed into the "Detroit Flyer", a passenger train bound for that American city. Though
the rate of speed of each train at the time of
impact at Streetsville Junction was minimal, one of
the cars in which many of the 48th Highlanders
were travelling was very old and completely
demolished in the collision. Two Highlanders were
killed outright and thirty more injured. In tribute
to the deceased soldiers, Privates Mac Murdock
and John Bannatyne, a special monument was prepared for the regiment's plot. This monument,
which has subsequently had the regiment's battle
honours inscribed on it, was moved in 1969 to a
more prominent location on the main road into the
cemetery a few yards east of Mount Pleasant Road.

# John Joseph Kelso

**# 165, plot 18, lot 33**

*A* native of Dundalk, Ireland, where he was born in 1864, J. J. Kelso emigrated to Toronto with his family in 1874. He was educated at Ryerson Public School and Jarvis Collegiate after which he obtained a job as a printer, first with the *Mail* and then the World newspapers. Kelso went on to become a reporter with the World for three years moving over to the *Globe* where he worked until 1902. It was as a reporter that he saw, first-hand, the cruel treatment afforded both youngsters and animals throughout the city. Following an address to the Canadian Institute, during which Kelso revealed various examples of what he had witnessed to a shocked audience, Kelso sought out supporters and in February of 1887 helped establish the Toronto Humane Society. Twenty-three-year-old Kelso became the new organization's first Secretary. At first, the Humane Society also looked after children, but in 1890 Kelso organized the Childrens' Aid Society of which he was elected President. In addition, Kelso was responsible for the province's Adoption Act, the Children of Unmarried Parents Act, the Alexandra School for Girls and several other child welfare projects including school dental services and the Toronto Playground Association. Kelso helped the provinces of Manitoba, Saskatchewan and British Columbia set up similar acts and programs. At the personal request of President Theodore Roosevelt, Kelso addressed the White House sponsored Child Welfare Conference in 1906. On September 30, 1935, at the age of seventy-one, John Joseph Kelso died at the home of his daughter, 31 Delavan Avenue in the Village of Forest Hill.

 # Robert Falconer

## # 166, plot 18, lot 268

*C*anada was a little less than five months away from Confederation when Robert Alexander Falconer was born in the same city in which the country was born, Charlottetown, Prince Edward Island. His birthdate was February 10, 1867. He obtained his early education in Trinidad, where his father was minister of the Presbyterian Church. He furthered his education in England, Scotland and on the continent. He lectured at Pinehill Theological College in Halifax, becoming Principal in 1904.

Three years later, he was appointed the University of Toronto's fifth President, a position he held for a quarter-of-a-century retiring due to health problems in 1932. It was during his univer-

245

MOUNT PLEASANT
CEMETERY

sity tenure that the University of Toronto was modernized and such new structures as Convocation Hall, Hart House and the Banting Institute were erected. Falconer was knighted by King George V in 1917, and also took a leading part in the creation of the United Church of Canada in 1925. Falconer died at his residence, 81 Glengowan Road, on November 4, 1943.

# John McIntosh Lyle

#167, plot 18, lot 279

*T*hough born in Belfast, Ireland in 1872, Lyle grew up in Hamilton, Ontario, where his father, a Presbyterian Minister had been assigned a small congregation. While living in Hamilton, Lyle's father established a small art school which his son attended. The young man showed such talent that he was enrolled in the Yale Art School and the Ecole des Beaux Arts in Paris, France. Having completed his schooling, Lyle practiced architecture for fourteen years in New York City before returning to Toronto, in 1907. Some of his local works include the Royal Alexandra Theatre, Runnymede Library, the original Toronto Stock Exchange building on Bay Street and (with others) Union Station. As consulting architect to the Civic Improvement Commission of 1911, Lyle was responsible for the routing of the Prince Edward Viaduct across the Don Valley. John Lyle won recognition amongst his peers for his use of distinctly Canadian motifs of flora, fauna and marine life in his industrial designs. Lyle died at his residence, 19 Avondale Road, on December 19, 1905.

# Thomas Rennie

# 168, plot 19, lot 68

*B*orn in Markham, Ontario on December 14, 1868, Rennie was educated at various Toronto public schools. When his father William Rennie retired in 1889 from the large seed business he had established, his three sons stepped in, with Thomas eventually assuming the presidency. In addition to his business interests, Rennie was one of the province's best and most ardent curlers and skipped numerous championship teams. In 1930, Rennie was appointed as a Toronto Harbour Commissioner becoming Chairman of the Board in 1936. He resigned after a total of seventeen years. In 1951, and in tribute to this popular businessman and devoted servant of the waterfront, the Toronto Transportation Commission named their newly constructed ferry boat *Thomas Rennie*. On August 4, 1952, Thomas Rennie died at the age of eighty-three.

MOUNT PLEASANT
CEMETERY

# William J. Stewart

#169, plot 19, lot 67

*W*illiam Stewart was born on Manning Avenue in west central Toronto in 1889. Little is known of his early life other than because of family financial problems, he was forced to leave school before graduating. Stewart entered municipal politics in 1924 and was elected Alderman for Ward 5. He held the position for the next six years and in 1931 entered the mayoralty race. He was successful in defeating the incumbent Sam McBride (PLOT D, SEC 20, LOT 8) by a mere 313 votes. Stewart continued to occupy the Mayor's chair until he retired at the end of his 1934 term. After two years out of public office, he contested the Ontario Conservative Party leadership, but finished third. In 1938, he was elected to the Provincial Legislature and appointed Speaker of the House in 1944. Stewart resigned the position in 1947 after a heated dispute with one of the provincial ministers and then was defeated in the 1948 general election by a C.C.F. candidate. He returned to the Legislature in 1951 and remained a provincial Member until defeated in 1959. Stewart was always interested in the city's history and was Mayor during Toronto's ambitious centennial celebrations in 1934. He was also a member of the Toronto Historical Committee and chairman of the Toronto Historical Board in 1969. In private business, Stewart was owner and President of Bates and Dodds, a long-time Toronto funeral home. William Stewart died on September 28, 1969, at the age of eighty after a brief illness.

 # George McCullagh

### # 170, plot 20, lot 67

*B*orn on March 6, 1905 in London, Ontario, the son of a well-meaning but sporadically employed carpenter, young George McCullagh was forced to leave high school before graduation to seek employment so he could help subsidize the meager family income. His first job, not counting that of delivering newspapers, was in a branch of the old Merchant's Bank in London. He soon grew tired of counting someone else's money and accepted a position as financial reporter at the *Globe* newspaper office in Toronto. His flair for the world of stocks and bonds soon saw him working in a brokerage office. It wasn't long after that he opened his own firm and soon became a director of Mining Corporation.

249

At the age of twenty-five, George McCullagh was a millionaire. One day he had the good fortune to be introduced to mining magnate and publisher of the *Globe* newspaper, William Henry Wright. Soon McCullagh was working for Wright and in 1936 was given $1,300,000 by the publisher to buy his newspaper operation. Within months McCullagh had latched on to another newspaper when he purchased the *Globe*'s arch-rival, the *Mail and Empire* for $2,020,000. The young newspaper tycoon brought his two papers together under one name, the *Globe and Mail*. A dozen years later, he added a third paper to his collection with the purchase of the *Evening Telegram* from the John Ross Robertson estate for $3,610,000. The December 1, 1948 edition of the newspaper, published with a slightly different and more succinct title, *The Telegram*, featured forty-three-year-old George McCullagh's name as publisher.

In addition to being the publisher of two of the country's most influential newspapers, McCullagh was also a director of several large mining concerns as well as being on the Board of Governors of the University of Toronto, the National Sanitarium Association, Maple Leaf Gardens and the Advisory Board of the Salvation Army. He was also a great philanthropist, giving large amounts of money to both the Toronto General Hospital and Hospital for Sick Children. Early in 1952, McCullagh's health began to fail. He suffered two heart attacks and, just when it looked as if he was on the road to full recovery, a third attack proved fatal. George McCullagh died on August 6, 1952 at the age of forty-seven at his Thornhill, Ontario estate. This estate is now the home of the famous Shouldice Clinic (see SECTION 26, PLOT 1).

# Arthur P. Coleman

## # 171, plot 20, lot 98

*T*he use of a large boulder from the Canadian Shield as a memorial headstone at Arthur Coleman's grave is most fitting in that Quebec-born University of Toronto professor spent many years exploring, surveying and mapping both Northern Ontario and the Canadian Rockies. Coleman served as president of the Royal Society of Canada, the Geological Society of America and the Royal Canadian Institute. He received the Victoria Medal from the prestigious Royal Geographical Society in 1933. He died at the age of eighty-six on February 28, 1939.

**MOUNT PLEASANT CEMETERY**

# Owen Staples

# 172, plot 21, sec 31, lot 43

*B*orn in the village of Stoke-sub-Hamdon, Somersetshire, England in 1866, young Staples emigrated to Hamilton, Canada with his parents when he was just six. He attended a private boys school in that city before moving to Rochester, New York with his mother and the rest of the family after his father died. Not long after, his mother too died and Owen was left to fend for himself. One day he obtained a job as messenger boy for the Rochester Art Club where he became fascinated with the various works of art on display in the club's galleries. Staples then began to study art and had further training at the Philadelphia Academy and at the Art Students' League in New York City. In 1885, he returned to Toronto and obtained employment with the the *Evening Telegram* newspaper. For more than sixty years, his cartoons and other forms of art work could be found in the city's most popular newspaper. Staples was also responsible for illustrating the six volume edition of *Telegram* owner John Ross Robertson's Landmarks of Toronto. Many of Staples' drawings of an earlier Toronto can be found throughout Toronto City Hall. Owen Staples died at his residence, 60 Hogarth Avenue on December 6, 1949 at the age of eighty-three.

 # David Archibald

#173, plot 21, lot 57

*B*orn in Ireland in 1842, Archibald was nineteen years old when he "signed on" with the Royal Irish Constabulary. In 1864, he resigned, emigrated to Toronto, where he joined the Toronto Police Department in 1865. After twenty-one years on the job, Archibald was appointed Staff Inspector, heading up the newly created Morals Division where he received the unofficial title of "first guardian of the city's moral welfare". His department was given the responsibility of "suppressing immorality in the city, to prevent the holding of prize cock and dog fights and a hundred-and-one other infractions of the law". In 1907, the six-foot-three policeman, dubbed "the moral man", was promoted to the rank of Chief Inspector and six years later to Deputy Chief.

Archibald retired in 1918 at the age of seventy-six, after fifty-two years of service. Early in 1938 he was stricken with pneumonia and died from resulting complications on January 15, 1938.

MOUNT PLEASANT
CEMETERY

# Edward Frederick Clarke

## # 174, plot 20, sec 20, lot 16

*A* native of Bailieboro, County Cavan, Ireland, Edward Clarke was educated in his hometown, coming to Toronto in 1864 at the age of fourteen where he was apprenticed to the printing trade. He worked for a time in the city's Globe printing office, but when the printers' strike of 1872 put hundreds of printers out of work. Clarke, the instigator, was put in jail. On his release, he became Editor, then Manager of the Orange Sentinel, the newspaper of the Orange Order. In 1886, he was elected to the provincial legislature where he remained until 1894. While sitting as an M.P.P., Clarke also served as Mayor of Toronto for a total of four successive years, 1888 to 1891. In 1894, Clarke entered the wonderful world of federal politics, when he won the seat for West Toronto a riding he continued to hold right up to his death at his residence at 358 Markham Street on March 3, 1905. The Clarke memorial marker was given by the McKinley Loyal Orange Lodge 275 and dedicated on October 20, 1905.

# George Weston

## # 175, plot 19, lot 26 & 27

**B**orn in Oswego, New York on March 23, 1864, Weston came to Canada with his parents as a small boy and settled in Toronto. At the age of eighteen, he was apprenticed to a local baker and in 1882, the industrious young man bought the business. With one horse and wagon, Weston became baker, deliveryman and bookkeeper. In 1911, his business and two other local bakeries were bought out and a new company called Canada Bread established.

As part of the deal, Weston was prevented from making and selling bread for ten years, so he moved into the biscuit business. After a period of time in England, where he learned how to make biscuits the British way, Weston returned to Toronto and established a new bakery on Bathurst Street and quickly introduced Torontonians to biscuits and cakes, English style. Weston also served as an Alderman for Ward Four during the period 1910 to 1913. George Weston died on April 6, 1924.

# Belt Line Railway

*I*n the late 1880s, Toronto, a city of less than 170,000 citizens, underwent a severe attack of growing pains. With more people flocking to "the Queen City", there soon became a desperate need for increased housing accommodation. In an effort to cash in on this land boom a group of prominent Toronto businessmen got together on July 16, 1889 and established the Toronto Belt Land Corporation, a syndicate that was ready, willing and able to develop and subdivide large parcels of land north of the city. These parcels would then be sold to Torontonians wishing to live outside the city in the beautiful "highlands of Toronto", as the syndicate's brochure promoted in picture and prose.

*Station at Moore Park*

Key to this suburban development north of city limits was a steam railway line that would encircle the city as far north as the properties being offered for sale by the syndicate. In 1890, Messrs. Hendrie and Manning, railway contractors, began construction of a loop of tracks that started at the old Union Station near the foot of Bay Street, ran east to the valley of the Don, then north to just above Bloor Street, where it headed off to the northwest through Silver Valley crossing under Moore Avenue (named for John T. Moore, Managing Director of the Belt Land Corporation who also gave his name to Moore Park and who is interred in Mount Pleasant Cemetery, PLOT 2, LOT 5) into the still virtually undeveloped grounds of Mount Pleasant Cemetery.

The plan to run track through the cemetery grounds met with stiff opposition from the Toronto General Burying Ground Trustees. Research indicates that it wasn't until cemetery lot owners had been convinced by both the directors of the syndicate and real estate experts that the line would be beneficial could work start through the cemetery property.

Once inside the cemetery grounds, the line curved westerly to eventually skirt along the north side of the property crossing Yonge Street on a steel bridge (which still stands just south of the Yonge and Merton Street intersection). The line then continued in a northwesterly direction, crossing under Eglinton Avenue, then continued westerly to a point near today's Caledonia Avenue. Here it joined the Grand Trunk's Northern Division trackage, running back to the waterfront, then east to Union Station. In total, it formed a belt of railway track some sixteen miles in length.

At the same time, the syndicate also constructed a much shorter Humber belt loop to serve Lambton, Swansea and Parkdale. Equipment on both routes was steam powered and both lines had provision for carrying freight.

A special inspection trip for company directors was held on October 14, 1891, with regularly scheduled commuter service starting on July 30 of the following year. Unfortunately, just as the Belt Line Railway started, so did a major downturn in the land boom on which the syndicate directors were relying for the success of their venture. The large numbers of people who, it was hoped, would take advantage of the Belt Land Corporation's suburban properties and the commuter line that would get them to work and home each night never materialized.

As a result, the innovative Belt Line Railway only operated for a brief twenty-seven months. On November 17, 1894, all service was terminated. The rolling stock reverted back to the Grand Trunk Railway and the corporation was dissolved, with many of the directors losing large amounts of money.

Several decades later, the City of Toronto's Planning Commissioner Tracy LeMay came up with an idea to construct a high speed "trafficway" that would connect the new cross-waterfront highway (today's Lake Shore Boulevard East) with Mount Pleasant Road north of Merton Street. Part of this trafficway would utilize the old Belt Line right-of-way through cemetery grounds.

To permit access to the east end of the cemetery property, should this thoroughfare be built, the Trustees of the cemetery ordered that a bridge be constructed over the former Belt Line Railway right-of-way. The Mount Pleasant Cemetery bridge, designed by prominent Canadian bridge engineer Frank Barber in collaboration with the architectural firm of Wickson and Gregg, opened in 1929.

For various reasons, Lemay's trafficway was never built and the Trustees were left with a bridge across nothing. Eventually, the structure deteriorated to such an extent that the bridge was demolished. A commemorative plaque can still be found on the wall of the old bridge's west approach.

# Mepham Gardens

*W*hen Edward H. Mepham died in 1976, he bequeathed a sizeable sum of money to the trustees of Toronto Trust Cemeteries to be used "for the beautification of Mount Pleasant Cemetery". One product of this bequest is the Mepham Pool and Gardens which were completed in the early 1980s. Income from the Mepham Trust continues to provide funds for the ongoing beautification of Mount Pleasant Cemetery. Edward H. Mepham is buried in SECTION 50, LOT 793.

 # Wallace Gordon Chalmers
### # 176, plot 23, lot 19B

*B*orn in Toronto on August 23, 1923, Wallace Chalmers attended Crescent School in Rosedale. As a youngster, Chalmers displayed a special fascination with automobiles and trucks and would frequently be deeply engrossed in drawing not just the vehicles, but more specifically, their intricate suspension systems. So after a short military career, it wasn't surprising that the talented young man would join the Direct-Winters trucking company where he could gain practical experience in the world of transportation. In 1945, Chalmers

returned to school attending the University of Toronto where he graduated with a degree in mechanical engineering in 1950.

Some years later, Chalmers perfected and patented a unique rubber suspension system for trucks and trailers. In 1970, Chalmers established Chalmers Suspensions International, Limited to manufacture and distribute his creation. The company was subsequently sold to the ARMBRO Group, a prominent Canadian highway construction firm, and Wallace Chalmers was retained as consultant. Always interested in the successful integration of engineering and design, Chalmers made large financial grants to the University of Waterloo and to St. Michael's Hospital. A special professorship in medicine, with emphasis on engineering design in treatment techniques was established at the latter institution. In 1985, Chalmers was awarded the Canadian Award for Excellence in Engineering.

At the time of his death, Chalmers, who was afflicted with bone cancer, was working on an innovative new wheelchair equipped with a special suspension that would make getting around easier for those with bone and neurological diseases. Wallace Chalmers died on September 25, 1987 at the age of sixty-four. The unusual Chalmers memorial stone, sculpted in the form of a large radial truck tire was designed by Erwin Hopp and carved out of African black granite by a Quebec monument company.

 # Frank Stollery

### # 177, sec 27, lot 197

*B*orn in the Village of Yorkville in 1879, Stollery attended school until the age of fourteen, at which

time he quit to learn how to cut shirts and ties. By the time he was twenty he was a foreman cutter in a Montreal clothing factory and was earning $12 a week. In 1900, Stollery joined the Royal Canadian Regiment and a year later returned to civilian life and opened his own haberdashery shop on Yonge Street just south of Bloor using $1,000 he had borrowed from his father to finance the venture. Years later, he moved to the southwest corner of Yonge and Bloor where he remained active in the retail clothing profession until he retired in 1968. The business that Stollery started in 1901, though now owned by interests outside his immediate family, is still very active.

During his younger years, Stollery was active in municipal politics, being elected senior Alderman for the local ward in 1923. He also helped establish the Yonge-Bloor-Bay Businessmen's Association, which is still going strong. Frank Stollery died at his North Toronto residence, 32 Teddington Park Avenue, on January 1, 1971.

 # Henry Houliston
## # 178, sec 27, lot 33

*I*n 1909, a livery company owned by Scottish-born Charles Verral introduced Torontonians to the taxicab and at the wheel of the city's first "horseless carriage for hire" ("Call Verral Livery at MAIN 123 to order yours") was twenty-eight-year-old Henry "Scotty" Houliston. He was also the first cab driver to drive from Toronto to New York City. His fare was a local hotel keeper and the trip took two weeks. When the pair arrived in New York they were feted at a City Hall reception. Henry Houliston, who resided at 119 Yorkville Avenue, died of blood poisoning at St. Joseph's Hospital on December 27, 1933.

# E. L. Ruddy
## # 179, sec 27, lot 217

*B*orn in Holyoke, Massachusetts and educated in Los Angeles, California, Ernest L. Ruddy came to Toronto in 1894 at the age of twenty-four. He was an advertising representative for several Canadian publications until he established his own outdoor advertising company in 1903 which became the largest in the country. During the First World War, Ruddy was active in the various Victory Loan campaigns and it was his suggestion that led to the first tank ever seen in Canada being brought to this country to bolster one such drive. In 1929, he sold his interest in E. L. Ruddy and Company for a million dollars and retired. Ruddy remained active in the National Sanitarium Association, serving as President of the organization from 1935 to 1949 and was one of the first to recommend free X-rays of the entire population to stop the spread of tuberculosis, a worrisome disease at the time. Ruddy died at his Balmoral Avenue residence on November 23, 1954, at the age of eighty-four.

**MOUNT PLEASANT CEMETERY**

# Earle Shouldice

## # 180, sec 26, plot 1

*B*orn in Chesley, Ontario, Shouldice graduated in medicine from the University of Toronto in 1916. He taught clinical medicine for a quarter-of-a-century before establishing the Shouldice Clinic. His interest in the treatment of hernias developed during the Second World War when, as a consulting physician to the Canadian Army, he was surprised by the number of otherwise fit young men who couldn't join the army because of their hernias. Dr. Shouldice began to operate on them free and after the war opened the first Shouldice Clinic in a six-room house on Church Street in downtown Toronto.

Soon the extremely successful treatment methods used by Dr. Shouldice became known far and wide, and it became necessary to find more expansive quarters for the clinic. In 1953, the doctor purchased the Bayview Avenue home of the late George McCullagh (SECT 20, LOT 67) in the Toronto suburb of Thornhill, including 135-acres of adjacent land, for $250,000 and converted it into the new Shouldice Clinic. Since 1945, more than 200,000 patients have received hernia operations at the Shouldice Clinic. Dr. Earle Shouldice succumbed to a heart attack at his Bayview Avenue clinic on August 20, 1965, at the age of seventy-four.

# Air Canada Flight 621 Memorial

### # 181, sec 24, lot 1

*E*arly Sunday morning on July 5, 1970, Air Canada's Montreal to Los Angeles via Toronto flight 621, dubbed the "California Galaxy," was making its final approach to Toronto International Airport's runway 32. As the four-engine DC-8-63 jet cleared the end of the runway, it suddenly dropped, hitting the tarmac with a stomach-wrenching thud, rebounded, powered up and roared into the morning sky desperately seeking a second try. Unknown to the flight crew, the outboard engine on the right wing had broken off and cartwheeled down the runway. Now working with just three engines, the captain was able to keep the plane in the air for another few minutes before it crashed into a farmer's field north of the airport. All 109 people on board flight 621 were killed.

A special memorial service was held on this spot at Mount Pleasant Cemetery on July 30, 1970, and in May of the following year a large memorial stone was erected. It is inscribed with the names of all 109 victims. A total of forty-nine identified and three unidentified victims of the ill-fated flight 621 are buried here.

**MOUNT PLEASANT CEMETERY**

# Alvan Sherlock Mathers

# 182, sec 26, lot 74

*A* graduate of the University of Toronto, Mathers was born in Aberfoyle, Ontario on July 16, 1895, and educated at schools in Hagersville and Thorold, Ontario. He began his architectural practice in 1919, forming a partnership with Eric W. Haldenby (PLOT 26, LOT 94) two years later. Some of the firm's best known Toronto works include the Imperial Oil Building on St. Clair Avenue West, the United States Consulate and University Club, both on University Avenue, the Sigmund Samuel Canadiana Building on Queen's Park Crescent West, the Bank of Nova Scotia at the northeast corner of King and Bay Streets, and the David Dunlap Observatory north of the city. Alvan Mathers died at his 28 Beechwood Avenue home in Willowdale on January 27, 1965.

# Matthew James Boylen

# 183, sec 26, lot 3

*B* orn in Toronto, Matthew James Boylen moved with his mother and father to an Alberta homestead. Not content with this way of life, when

266

he reached the age of twelve, young Matthew returned to Toronto and as a teenager became a prospector in Northern Ontario. This enterprising gentleman, who never completed grade school, was awarded three honorary degrees including a Doctorate of Civil Law from the University of New Brunswick. His most notable venture was the one hundred million dollar Brunswick Mining and Smelting Corporation which in 1969, the year before Boylen's death, produced over $43 million in lead and zinc. He also established Advocate Mines, an asbestos operation at Baie Verte, Newfoundland. He was also an ardent outdoorsman and enthusiastic breeder of fine thoroughbreds. Matthew James Boylen died at his Kingsway Crescent home on July 7, 1970.

 # Frederick Banting

#184, sec 29, lot 29

*B*orn in Alliston, Ontario in 1891, Frederick Banting received his early education in that small town, west of Toronto. Moving to Toronto in 1911, he attended Victoria College graduating in medicine from the University of Toronto in late 1916. He served overseas during the First World War winning the Military Cross and was wounded in France while serving as medical officer with the 44th Battalion, Canadian Expeditionary Force.

In the years following the war, Banting gave up a promising medical practice in London, Ontario to pursue his research at the University of Toronto to find a cure for diabetes. In 1921, assisted by Charles Best and J. B. Collip and under

*Dr. Banting with his assistant, Charles Best, and one of their "patients".*

the supervision of J. R. R. Macleod, Banting managed to isolate and purify insulin which, while not a cure, helped diabetic patients live a near normal life.

Banting and Macleod were awarded the Nobel Prize for the most important medical discovery of 1923. Annoyed that Best was overlooked by the selection committee, Banting decided to share his half of the $11,200 award with his colleague and friend. Following Banting's lead, Macleod did the same with Collip.

On February 21, 1941, while on "a mission of high national and scientific importance" to Great Britain, the aircraft in which Banting was a passenger crashed near Musgrave Harbour, Newfoundland. The doctor soon died of his injuries and was brought back to Toronto for burial on March 4, 1941, following a service at the University of Toronto's Convocation Hall and a funeral procession to Mount Pleasant Cemetery.

# Ferdinand Herbert Marani

## # 185, plot 29, lot 195

*B*orn in Vancouver, British Columbia on August 8, 1893, Marani was educated at Ridley College in St. Catharines and at the University of Toronto. As a young man, he went overseas during the First World War and served with the Royal Canadian Horse Artillery, attaining the rank of Lieutenant-Colonel. Returning to Toronto after the war, Marani embarked on what was to be an illustrious architectural career.

Working by himself at first, Marani's first commissions were almost entirely residential. In 1924, he took in his first partner, thus beginning a series of name changes by which the company has been known and recognized world-wide ever since - Marani and Paisley (1924-5), Marani, Lawson and Paisley (1926-8), Marani and Lawson (1929), Marani, Lawson and Morris (1930-40), Marani and Morris (1941-58), Marani, Morris and Allan (1959-64), Marani, Rounthwaite and Dick (1964-80). Since 1981, the same company has operated under the name Rounthwaite, Dick and Hadley. Some of Marani's most notable Toronto works include the Medical Arts Building on Bloor Street West (1928-29), St. Joseph's Hospital on The Queensway (1936), the I.O.O.F Building (later Metropolitan Toronto Police headquarters) (1951), Manufacturers Life Assurance addition on Bloor Street East (1953), the Crown Life Building on Bloor Street East (1956) and the Confederation Life (1954-56) Building on Bloor Street East, the Bank of Canada Building (1955), the Maclean Hunter Building addition (1961) and the new

**MOUNT PLEASANT CEMETERY**

Courthouse (1964-66), the latter three on University Avenue.

During the Second War, Marani enlisted in the R.C.A.F, rising to the rank of Group Captain. At the end of the war, he sat on a number of planning and housing committees. Marani was also appointed a Trustee of the Toronto General Burial Grounds (now Toronto Trust Cemeteries), a position he held until his death on July 18, 1971.

# Jack Dennett
## # 186, sec 28, plot 2330

*O*ne of the best known voices on Canadian radio, Dennett was born in Calgary, Alberta in 1916. His first "on-air" job was at the age of sixteen with Calgary radio station CFCA where he was paid the princely weekly wage of $4. Over the years, he worked for various radio stations and was hired by Toronto's CFRB in 1943. Dennett broadcast the 8 a.m. and 6:30 p.m. newscasts for a total of twenty-six years, during which time he never missed a scheduled newscast. It was said that Dennett had more listeners than any other newscaster in the entire country. He was also known for his "Hockey Night in Canada" television appearances. Dennett died on August 27, 1975 of cancer.

 # Charles H. Best
### # 187, sec 29, lot 480

*A*t the age of twenty-two, medical researcher Charles Best joined Dr. Frederick Banting in the quest to find a cure for diabetes. Born in West Pembroke, Maine in 1899, Best moved to Toronto with his Nova Scotian-born father and mother early in the new century. It was while studying physiology at the University of Toronto that the young man was approached by Banting to assist the latter in diabetes research. In 1921, the pair discovered insulin, and soon thereafter Best became the Director of the Insulin Division of Connaught Laboratories.

Best obtained his medical degree in 1925. Following Banting's untimely death in 1941, Dr. Best became head of the Banting and Best Department of Medical Research. Dr. Charles Best died at the Toronto General Hospital on March 31, 1978.

# S. S. Noronic Memorial

## # 188, sec 29, lot 182, 183 and 184

*I*t had just turned six o'clock on the evening of Friday, September 16, 1949 when the shimmering black-hulled Canada Steamship Lines passenger steamer *Noronic* glided smoothly through Toronto's Western Gap and edged up to her berth near the foot of Yonge Street. Within a few minutes she was moored securely and passengers began to make their way ashore. *Noronic* was about halfway through her last cruise of the 1949 fall season, a leisurely cruise from Cleveland, Ohio and Detroit, Michigan to Prescott, Ontario and the Thousand Islands, with a brief sightseeing stopover in Toronto. On board were 524 passengers and 171 crew members. All of the passengers being American citizens.

At about 2:30 a.m., a late returning passenger noticed smoke billowing from under a linen locker door on "C" deck. He and one of the crew opened the door only to be met by a wall of flame. Together they attempted to douse the flames, but with little success. Eventually, an alarm was put in to the Toronto Fire Department, but by the time the first trucks arrived at the quayside, the once proud *Noronic* was enveloped in flames. Throughout the night, police, firemen and helpful citizens fought the stubborn blaze and helped rescue terrified passengers.

A final count of the dead, many of whom were charred beyond recognition, revealed that a total of 119 unfortunate souls had lost their lives in the worst disaster to have ever afflicted the City of Toronto. The identified remains were soon released for burial, most being returned to their American hometowns. On January 17, 1950, at a grave site purchased by the Province of Ontario, fifteen human bodies were interred, along with portions of another thirty-seven, plus a large quantity of human ashes. Five different faiths were represented at a moving ceremony in the presence of the Premier of Ontario Leslie Frost, Toronto Mayor Hiram McCallum, Chief of Police John Chisholm and Fire Chief Peter Herd.

# Alan Brown

#### # 189, sec 29, lot 178
#### (Fisher plot)

*B*orn in Clinton, Ontario in 1887, Alan Brown graduated in medicine from the University of Toronto with honours and then spent three years

at the Babies' Hospital in New York City. He did
his post-graduate work in several famous pediatric
hospitals throughout Europe, before returning to
Toronto where he joined the staff of the Hospital
for Sick Children, then on College Street.

Appalled at the hospital's high mortality rate,
the determined doctor was permitted to implement
radical changes and within a year the death rate
at the hospital was cut in half. He was soon
appointed the hospital's Physician-in-Chief. Dr.
Brown was also instrumental in forcing the
Provincial Government to pass compulsory pasteu-
rization legislation to help stop the incidence of
tuberculosis in children.

Perhaps Dr. Brown is best known for his
involvement in the development in a new cereal
mixture for children that contained vitamins and
mineral elements. Dr. Brown had hired the
product's co-creators, Doctors Theo Drake and Fred
Tisdall, to help him improve the situation in the
hospital wards and they came up with a revolutionary product they dubbed Pablum (from the Latin
"pabulum" meaning "food"). Pablum was responsible for saving thousands of youngsters from death
and disease. The royalties resulting from its sale
went to help further research at the hospital as well
as to assist in the financing of a new Hospital for
Sick Children on University Avenue that opened in
1951. Dr. Brown died on September 7, 1960.

# Eric Wilson Haldenby

## # 190, sec 26, lot 94

*T*oronto-born Haldenby was educated at Parkdale Collegiate and the University of Toronto and with the outbreak of war in 1914, graduated from the Officers Training Course with the rank of Lieutenant. He was awarded the Military Cross for his actions at Vimy Ridge in 1917.

After the war, Haldenby obtained his degree in architecture and in 1921, he and A. S. Mathers formed the architectural firm of Mathers and Haldenby, a company that was responsible for the design of many Toronto landmarks including the Bank of Nova Scotia Building at King and Bay Streets, the United States Consulate on University Avenue, the David Dunlap Observatory, the Charles H. Best Institute on College Street and many buildings on the University of Toronto grounds.

Throughout most of his life, Haldenby was closely associated with the 48th Highlanders of Canada joining that organization in 1915. He fought with the unit during the First World War and was promoted to the rank of Lieutenant-Colonel in 1939. Haldenby commanded the 48th overseas during the Second World War. He was responsible for the design of the 48th Highlanders Monument at the north end of Queen's Park that stands in memory of the eight hundred Highlanders from Toronto that made the supreme sacrifice. Haldenby was appointed Honourary Colonel of the 48th Highlanders of Canada in 1963. Eric Wilson Haldenby died in Sunnybrook Hospital on October 18, 1971, at the age of seventy-eight.

MOUNT PLEASANT
CEMETERY

# Jennie Smillie Robertson

# 191, sec 32, lot 501

*B*orn on a farm near Hensall, Ontario on February 10, 1878, Jennie Smillie's first job was as a teacher in Huron County. Out of her annual salary of $300, the young lady saved enough to enroll in the Ontario Medical College for Women at 291 Sumach Street, a few doors north of Gerrard Street. The college closed the following year, and classes were integrated into the University of Toronto's Medical School, all except for anatomy classes. (Many more years were to pass before both male and female students were study anatomy together, on the campus at least.) Since none of the city hospitals were yet ready to accept women doctors in 1909, after her graduation the thirty-one-year-old doctor was forced to intern in a Philadelphia hospital. Even after she returned to Toronto, the local hospitals were still reluctant to give her operating privileges.

In 1911, Dr. Smillie and several other female doctors banded together and opened the city's original Women's College Hospital in a rented house on Seaton Street. Canada's first woman surgeon didn't get married until shortly after her retirement. Then at the age of seventy she traded vows with childhood sweetheart Alex Robertson. Dr. Jennie Smillie Robertson died in a nursing home on February 26, 1981.

# Thomas W. Thompson

*# 192, sec 32, lot 864*

*B*orn in 1914 next door to Toronto's famous Casa Loma, where his father worked as a grounds-keeper, young Tommy Thompson obtained after-school employment looking after the gardens at Toronto Trust Cemeteries' Prospect Cemetery on St. Clair Avenue West. After graduating from high school, Thompson enrolled at the Ontario Agricultural College in Guelph and having completed courses there in 1936 was hired as a gardener at Mount Pleasant Cemetery.

277

**MOUNT PLEASANT CEMETERY**

With the outbreak of war, Thompson joined the R.C.A.F. and trained as a navigator-bombardier. After the war, he spent some time in the Ontario Department of Education advising communities on the care of parks, arenas and playgrounds before becoming Parks Superintendent for the City of Port Arthur (now part of Thunder Bay), Ontario. Thompson returned to Toronto in 1955 and became the first Parks Commissioner for the newly established Metropolitan Toronto Parks Department, a position he held for more than twenty years. Soon after the new Metro Zoo in Scarborough opened, Thompson was appointed Director and helped "get the bugs" out of the new facility. Thompson retired in 1981, but kept busy serving on numerous committees and leading public walks around his beloved city. Some of his most popular forages were through Mount Pleasant Cemetery, where he loved to talk about the unique collection of trees and shrubs. Seventy-one-year-old Tommy Thompson died at the Western Hospital on March 1, 1985. Carved on his memorial stone is a likeness of Tommy's famous walking stick and the words that will always remind us of his love of parks and green spaces, "PLEASE WALK ON THE GRASS".

 # William James

# 193, sec 42, lot 321

*B*orn in the small village of Walsall near Wolverhampton, England in 1866, James and his young family emigrated to Toronto in 1906. He obtained work as an insurance agent, but soon gave it up to pursue his first love, photography.

James took photographs which he then sold for a
dollar or two to the city's seven daily newspapers.
He photographed not only the great, but the hum-
ble as well. He also captured many historic events
on film and is said to have been the first person to
photograph the city from the air. Several years
ago, the City of Toronto Archives acquired the William James' collection of photographs and nega-
tives, an invaluable compendium of the Toronto
"that used to be". After forty years as a freelance
photographer, James retired in 1940. He died at
the age of eighty-two on November 18, 1948.

**MOUNT PLEASANT
CEMETERY**

# Charlie Conacher

#194, sec 41, lot 351

*B*orn in Toronto on December 10, 1906, Charlie Conacher attended Jesse Ketchum Public School. He played hockey in the National Hockey League for a total of twelve seasons, nine with the Toronto Maple Leafs (1929-1938), his Leafs winning the Stanley Cup in 1931-32. Conacher led the League in scoring for four consecutive years, scoring his very first N.H.L. goal on his first shift as a rookie Maple Leaf rightwinger, November 14, 1929. Conacher was probably best known as a member of the famous "Kid Line" along with Joe Primeau and Harvey "Busher" Jackson. The total age of the trio when formed by Conn Smythe on December 7, 1929 was fifty-eight years.

Following his retirement from hockey in 1941, Conacher became a successful business-man and listed amongst his friends Dwight Eisenhower, Bob Hope and Bing Crosby. After a long bout with cancer, Charlie Conacher died at the Toronto General Hospital on January 30, 1968. The Conacher memorial stone is an intriguing work of art as are the Schlesinger (SECTION 36, LOT 1088) and Torokvey (SECTION 36, LOT 4100) memorials.

# H. Spencer Clark

## # 195, sec 43, lot 1

*A* born Torontonian, Spencer Clark graduated from the University of Toronto in 1924. By profession he was an electrical engineer, but secretly harboured a passion to establish an artistic centre for artists and craftsmen. Following his marriage to Rosa Breithaupt Hewetson in 1932, the two established the Guild of All Arts situated on forty acres of land on the brow of the Scarborough Bluffs, east of Toronto. Originally the Guild property and its fifteen bedroom manor house had been part of the General Harold Bickford estate. They invited artists to live and work on the estate and soon the Guild of All Arts was a haven for dozens of talented, but out-of-work artists.

In 1934, the manor house became a country inn and two years later, rooms were being rented by Rosa and Spencer to overnight guests. Following the end of the Second World War, during which time the inn had been taken over by the military, Spencer Clark began collecting pieces of old Toronto landmarks that were being torn apart as the city rushed to become a concrete jungle. Important fragments of more than sixty city landmarks can be found scattered around the Guild's park-like grounds.

Over the years, the Clarks increased their land holdings to almost ninety acres, eventually selling the inn and grounds to the Metro Toronto and Region Conservation Authority for safekeeping in 1978. The Guildwood Village residential community was developed on former Guild property. Rosa Clark died on July 7, 1981 at the age of ninety-two. Spencer, age eighty-two, passed away February 11, 1986.

MOUNT PLEASANT
CEMETERY

# Steele Basil

## # 196, sec 39, lot 69

*A*rriving in Toronto from his native Greece at the tender age of fourteen, it took Steele Basil just three years to open his first restaurant, the Green Lantern Tea Room on Bloor Street West. In 1936, Basil opened Steele's Tavern at 349 Yonge Street and for the next thirty-seven years it was one of the most popular restaurants in the city and one of the first to be licensed. In 1960, Basil introduced live entertainment. One of his first performers was an unknown twenty-one-year-old singer from Orillia, Ontario by the name of Gordon Lightfoot. Steele Basil died November 7, 1981 at the age of seventy-four.

# Glenn Gould

## # 197, sec 38, lot 1050

*B*orn in Toronto on September 25, 1932, Gould was able to read music at the age of three. Two years later, he was writing music and playing piano for neighborhood friends. Gould studied piano at the Toronto Conservatory of Music (after 1947 the Royal Conservatory of Music of Toronto) from 1943 to 1952. However, he made his debut as an organist, not a pianist, at the famous Eaton Auditorium on December 12, 1945. Gould went on

to become one of the world's most celebrated (and most eccentric) classical musicians. Throughout his adult life Glenn Gould remained an enigma, being both admired and hated by his peers, frequently at the same time. Nevertheless, Gould was and still is adored by his fans. In late September, 1982, Gould suffered a massive stroke and died at the Toronto General Hospital on October 4, 1982.

# George Alan MacLachlan
## # 198, sec 35, lot 25

*O*n May 7, 1944 the Canadian warship *H.M.C.S. Valleyfield* was torpedoed by German submarine *U-548* in the north Atlantic southeast of Cape Race, Newfoundland and sank within six minutes.

MOUNT PLEASANT
CEMETERY

One hundred-and-twenty-five of her crew were killed in the tragedy, *Valleyfield* was the first Canadian frigate and the tenth Canadian ship lost to enemy action since the start of the Second World War.

First reports had Lt. George Alan MacLachlan missing at sea. However, his body was never found and the young man is remembered on the MacLachlan family monument in Mount Pleasant with the words "LOST AT SEA ON THE *H.M.C.S. VALLEYFIELD*". George Alan MacLachlan was just one of 1,990 members of the Royal Canadian Navy who made the supreme sacrifice in the Second World War.

# Superintendents/Managers
# of Mount Pleasant Cemetery

1873-1888 Henry A. Engelhardt
1888-1889 Belhat Lawson
1889-1902 Henry Thompson
1902-1905 Jeffrey Foote
1905-1934 William H. Foord
1934-1948 J.H. Cunningham
1948-1980 Alan K. Clark
1980-1986 Glen E. Timney
1986-1989 Fraser Vey
1989-1990 Glen E. Timney
1990-      Wayne Ogden

**MOUNT PLEASANT**
**CEMETERY**

# Author's Acknowledgments

*S*taff of Toronto Trust Cemeteries; Michela DeVita, Brenda Rodrigue, Karen Ireland, Louise Winton, Angie Aquino, Jack Radecki, Glen Timney, Eric Tappenden and Bob Smith, Julie Kirsch and her staff at the Toronto Sun Library, Victor Russell and Patrick Cummins of the City of Toronto Archives, Johanne Pelletier and Major Lorraine Luxford of the Salvation Army, Rennie Graham, Howard Clark, Pleasance Crawford, Sally Coutts, Heinz Mueller, Al Navis and Tim Douglas. A special thanks to my wife, Yarmila who, as she has so many times before, helped me in a myriad of ways.